DOCUMENTARY STUDIES IN MODERN RUSSIAN POETRY Memoirs, biographies, and critical views, in newly translated editions, by and about the exceptional men and women of the early twentieth-century renascence in Russian poetry.

GENERAL EDITORS: Robert P. Hughes AND Simon Karlinsky

1. *The Diary of Valery Bryusov (1893–1905). With Reminiscences by V. F. Khodasevich and Marina Tsvetaeva.* Edited, Translated, and with an Introductory Essay by Joan Delaney Grossman. 1980.

2. Vladimir Zlobin. *A Difficult Soul: Zinaida Gippius.* Edited, Annotated, and with an Introductory Essay by Simon Karlinsky. 1980.

3. Andrei Bely. *Reminiscences of Alexander Blok.* Translated, Annotated, and with an Introductory Essay by Robert P. Hughes. 1981.

The Diary of
Valery Bryusov
(1893–1905)

Valery Bryusov against a studio backdrop,
photographed between 1908 and 1910.
Courtesy of the Institute of World Literature,
Academy of Sciences, USSR, Moscow.

The Diary of Valery Bryusov

(1893–1905)

WITH REMINISCENCES
BY V. F. Khodasevich
AND Marina Tsvetaeva

EDITED, TRANSLATED, AND WITH
AN INTRODUCTORY ESSAY BY
Joan Delaney Grossman

University of California Press
BERKELEY · LOS ANGELES · LONDON

University of California Press
Berkeley and Los Angeles, California

University of California Press, Ltd.
London, England

© 1980 by
The Regents of the University of California

Printed in the United States of America

1 2 3 4 5 6 7 8 9

Library of Congress Cataloging in Publication Data

Briusov, Valeriĭ I͡Akovlevich, 1873–1924.
　The diary of Valery Bryusov (1893–1905)

　(Documentary studies in modern Russian poetry)
　Bibliography: p.
　Includes index.
　　1. Brivsov, Valeriĭ I͡Akovlevich, 1873–1924—Diaries.
2. Brivsov, Valeriĭ I͡Akovlevich, 1873–1924—
Biography—Addresses, essays, lectures. 3. Poets,
Russian—20th century—Biography—Addresses, essays,
lectures.　I. Khodasevich, Vladislav Felit͡sianovich,
1886–1939.　II. T͡Svetaeva, Marina Ivanova Efron,
1892–1941.　III. Grossman, Joan Delaney.　IV. Title.
V. Series.
PG3453.B7Z524　　1980　　　891.784203 [B]　　　78-66013

ISBN 0-520-03858-4

Contents

Note on Transliteration	vii
Introduction	1
The Diary of Valery Bryusov	33
Reminiscences	147
From "Bryusov" by V. F. KHODASEVICH	149
From "Hero of Labor: Notes on Valery Bryusov" by MARINA TSVETAEVA	161
APPENDIX: Twenty-One Poems by Valery Bryusov	175
Glossary of Proper Names	205
Selected Bibliography	223
Index	229

Note on Transliteration

Russian names and words occurring in the text are spelled so as to facilitate pronunciation by readers who know no Russian. This system is also used for Russian personal proper names in the glossary. For the convenience of those who wish to consult Russian sources, the international scholarly system of transliteration is used in footnotes for Russian titles, in the glossary for the original names of Russian periodicals, and in the selected bibliography.

The Diary of
Valery Bryusov
(1893–1905)

Introduction

The surprising thing about the turn of the century in Russia, to paraphrase Martin Turnell on nineteenth-century France, is not that it was a profoundly fertile period for literature, but that the era should have produced literature at all. The age of the great Russian novels ended around 1880. Poetry, so marvellously rich before 1840, had been obscured and largely choked with dust stirred by the demand for social relevance, which extended through the 1870s. At the end of the century Russian society itself was in one of those troubled phases which history later calls transitional. Yet this state of affairs does not seem in retrospect to have hindered new developments greatly, and in some way may even have helped them.

Beginning roughly in 1845, Russian cultural life was dominated on the one hand by the great Realists and on the other by a determinedly civic-minded press. The momentum built up from mid-century by these two forces lasted for several decades, and during that time was too strong to allow entry from the West of the new and diametrically opposite trends arising there. These changes of sensibility and artistic direction which became prominent also from mid-century and most strongly in France found no noticeable resonance in contemporary Russia. That "human prototype of new experience," Baudelaire (so called by T. S. Eliot), was taken scant notice of there until the early 1890s. Symbolism arose in France in the mid-eighties on ground prepared by Baudelaire, by Gautier and the Parnassians. But there was nothing gradual or prepared about the revelation to Russian readers in the mid-nineties of the work of Verlaine, Rimbaud, and Mallarmé. Not even the surface of Russian culture had been rippled by those other movements in Western European literature and art which made for a rich half-century of esthetic experience leading into the spirit we call modern. All of this had to wait a favorable season for entry into Russia. Only near the end of the century did the opportunity occur. Despite the presence of Gorky, Chekhov, and the still redoubtable Leo Tolstoy, a period of cultural boredom had set in. At last some members of a new generation, hungry for new models, for new attitudes toward life and art, turned first of all to France. And at just that point the young Moscow poet Valery Bryusov decided to seize the moment, appointing himself organizer and leader of the new art in Russia.

Bryusov was not the first Russian Symbolist or Decadent (the terms were at first used interchangeably). It is not clear that he was technically a Symbolist at all. But for a time—perhaps a decade and a half—he appeared to be both founder of a school of poetry and leader of a literary movement. Acclaimed as Russia's greatest poet during a few years in the early 1900s, standard-bearer of Russian Symbolism and editor of its most prestigious journal, *The Balance,* recognized as "master" by Alexander Blok, Andrei Bely, and a host of lesser lights, friend and translator of Western poets like Emile Verhaeren, Bryusov rose high. Correspondingly, he had a long distance to fall. The fact that he did fall, by way of a gradual decline from authority after about 1912, is owing equally to the nature of the role he had assumed and to the limits of his poetic talent and the efflorescence of greater talents around him. Nevertheless, his career was a vivid one and of major significance for modern Russian poetry.

Bryusov made his pitch for fame by identifying himself with a movement. The new art—Symbolism, Decadence—seemed a necessity not only for Russia but for himself. Meaning to use his ascendance to establish higher poetic standards and to free poetry from the tedium of extraliterary demands, he both succeeded and failed. Some of the greatest Symbolists admitted their debt to Bryusov's art but rejected his restrictions on poetry's use. They insisted on its essentially theurgic nature and used it accordingly. Thus during its greatest years, the Symbolist movement, as personified by Blok, Bely, and Vyacheslav Ivanov, took a direction which Bryusov had not foreseen and which he violently disapproved of. Post-Symbolist poetry was to take still other unexpected turns in the work of Osip Mandelstam, Boris Pasternak, Vladimir Mayakovsky, Anna Akhmatova, and Marina Tsvetaeva, to mention the greatest. Their contributions to Russian poetry surpassed Bryusov's, nor were many of them inclined to lay wreaths at his poetic monument. In part that was owing to their evolution in a direction different from his. Perhaps it was also because he insisted on setting up his own monument and exacting so much tribute while at the peak of his fame.

Yet Bryusov undoubtedly deserves a wreath of some proportions. No man did more to bring about that change of atmosphere in Russian letters which determined the direction of coming decades. Nor was his poetry of mere passing value. Who was Bryusov as a poet? First of all, he was an innovator, a conscious reformer. The once glorious line of Pushkin had sunk to banality in the work of successors of less talent and little inspiration. The same, often elegiac, themes were sung repeatedly in the same rhythms, capped by the same rhymes. The rich infusion of Nekrasov's poetry at mid-century, full of popular themes and folk rhythms, had sunk to mere tendentious verse. The technical side of poetry in not advancing for decades had fallen back. Poetic language had grown anemic in the extreme by 1890. Of all this the young Bryusov was acutely aware. Especially he felt the presence of new themes to be sung. "What if I tried to write a treatise on spectral analysis couched in the language of Homer? . . . The same thing if I try to express *fin de siècle* sensations in Pushkin's language. Yes, Symbolism is necessary!"

His early, innovative attempts were often gauche, though sometimes striking. But adolescence once past, Bryusov appeared as a poet of power and individuality. His sense of language and form honed to the finest, he became recognized and diligently studied for his technical mastery by younger poets like Blok and Bely. (Blok was so captivated by Bryusov's 1903 volume *Urbi et orbi* that for a time he read it nightly. He wrote ecstatically to its author: "What will you do after *this?*") Bryusov's poetry was in fact a stunning phenomenon in the first years of the century. Thematically his work is marked by a wide range of imagination, a capacity for projecting himself into almost every kind of psychological experience, even the most extreme (a talent which, incidentally, Dostoevsky remarked in Bryusov's hero Edgar Allan Poe). He thus opened perspectives which his younger contemporaries did not neglect to explore.

As with most poets, some of Bryusov's work has lost its lustre over the decades. But some stands as high as ever it did. It was unfortunate for his enduring fame, though not for Russian poetry, that greater poets followed his lead so quickly. A further hindrance to his fame, ironically, was that very break with tradition which did so much immediately to revive Russian poetry. The break was not permanent. The poetry of Blok, to identify the voice which did most to mute Bryusov's, was felt as a fresh and vitalizing return to that tradition, and it had a strongly Russian ring. Bryusov's best poetry—much as this would have vexed him—may by comparison sound a shade alien to Russian ears. Thus, despite his importance to Russian poetry's development and his great veneration for and knowledge of Pushkin and other greats, his work has never become part of that canonical tradition which stems from Pushkin. (Indeed, he was chastised on all sides for his audacity in completing Pushkin's unfinished masterpiece *Egyptian Nights*.) Tyutchev, Fet, and Baratynsky, besides other nineteenth-century luminaries, influenced his poetry more strongly than Pushkin. And he did much to set these three before the eyes of his contemporaries. But for all his saturation in the tradition, Bryusov has never become an accepted part of it: his voice is not heard in the chorus.

Nonetheless, his innovations have resounded there. It was, after all, Bryusov who introduced or diffused themes new to Russian poetry, if not to readers of Baudelaire or Dostoevsky: the city, the terrors of modern life, the exotic, the erotic, and the perverse. While much of his poetry is traditional in form, he experimented fruitfully with rhyme, meter, rhythm, and sound pattern. But, beyond all this, Bryusov reopened Russia's window on Western poetry. (Renato Poggioli called him "a Peter the Great in miniature" who "gave a Russian voice to the poetry of France.") Translator of Mallarmé,

Verlaine, Maeterlinck, Verhaeren, and Poe, he preached by example to the Russian reading public and its poets his passionate belief that European literature was one. His years as moving spirit of *The Balance* were in part an effort to realize this belief, as far as Russia was concerned. Articles on contemporary writers abroad, foreign contributors and correspondents like René Ghil and Remy de Gourmont, illustrations by Aubrey Beardsley and Odilon Redon, title page and table of contents bilingual in Russian and French: the whole spirit informing the journal was European in the most modern sense, and Bryusov was in the forefront of the effort to make it so.

Yet withall, it was also Bryusov who, very early in his development, recognized the need to renew connections between modern Russian poetry and its native roots, both for the sake of craft and for the rich strains of philosophical poetry there contained. Even before his reputation as poetic innovator was established, Bryusov was grubbing in old journals, publishing articles and documents in the historical journal *Russian Archive,* and planning a large work to be called *History of the Russian Lyric.* Though this last was never completed, his archive contains much prepared material. Furthermore, he published during his career eighty-two pieces relating to Pushkin, to say nothing of work on a number of other important figures. Perhaps one of the reasons a brash young group of Futurists, including Mayakovsky, could write in 1912 that they wanted to "throw Pushkin, Dostoevsky, Tolstoy, et al., et al., overboard from the Ship of Modernity" was that the tradition had been reestablished and newly understood by the generation before them. Rebel they might, but the reservoir of strength was there. For this no small thanks was owing to Bryusov.

1

The trajectory of Bryusov's career is readily traced. From 1894 to 1904 he was busy establishing himself as poet and as leader of the new school, or specifically of the Moscow branch of it. Contrasting the Moscow and Petersburg variants of early twentieth-century Decadence, the Symbolist poet Zinaida Gippius noted that Petersburg Decadents were esthetes, pallid snobs who drew their inspiration entirely from the West and feared any lapse from *le bon ton.* Moscow Decadence on the other hand was hearty, outrageous, a native flower of sorts, vital and capable of development. As poets, however, both groups formed on rather unpromising native ground. Poetic craft in particular had gone badly to seed. Like nearly everyone else the young Valery Bryusov admired Nadson, favorite of an age which had lost any taste. But he soon turned to other models. His progress is traceable through a grossly imitative, puerile, Byronic stage to a point where he surely panted for new inspiration. At that propitious moment, the September 1892 number of the prestigious liberal Petersburg journal *Messenger of Europe* printed an article on French Symbolism. From that point *Symbolism* and *Decadence* became not so much words in Bryusov's vocabulary as banners to be hoisted. His March 4, 1893, diary declaration of intent to lead Decadence in Russia reflected his conviction that change was overdue and that any change was better than none—provided, of course, that he was its leader.

With characteristic brashness and vigor, Bryusov put

intent into action. With the help of more pseudonyms than contributing authors, he published in 1894 and 1895 three slim volumes of *Russian Symbolists*. He later wrote that his discovery of Mallarmé, Verlaine, and Baudelaire in the early 1890s opened a new world to him. Many of his verses in *Russian Symbolists* explored the possibilities of a "poetry of suggestion." But his efforts drew both indignation and ridicule. His "golden-tinted fairies / in a satin garden" bearing "incomprehensible vases" were promptly unmasked by Vladimir Solovyov as "female persons bathing behind a fence," using metal basins. And his famous one-liner "O cover your pale legs" became a shibboleth for opponents of the new art. ("I simply wanted to experiment in Russian with the form [used by the Romans for epigrams or epitaphs]," he later explained.)

Liberally padded with translations from Verlaine, Maeterlinck, Mallarmé, and Edgar Allan Poe, these three volumes launched Bryusov into the public arena with the only kind of success he could have expected, a *succès de scandale*. At the end of his 1894 diary he wrote with something like pride, "At the beginning of this notebook no one knew of me, but now all the journals tear me to bits." Parodies of some of his more extreme poems by the respected poet-philosopher Vladimir Solovyov accompanied a caustically funny review of the new phenomenon. Solovyov's remark that "if Mr. Bryusov is no more than fourteen years old, he may turn into a decent poet, or he may not," put Bryusov down badly. But at least his name was now known. The critical failure of his own first collection *Chefs d'oeuvre* in 1895 was perhaps less expected and therefore less bearable. Early in that year he wrote to a Petersburg friend that "these will be masterpieces, not of my own poetry (in the future I will doubtless write even more important things), but masterpieces of contemporary poetry. . . ." Upon the book's appearance in late August, however, he was anticipating critical reaction: "What kind of masterpieces are these, I ask myself, miserable jingles, pretensions and nothing more." Nonetheless, he defiantly published a revised and augmented edition in March 1896.

In the preface to the second edition Bryusov characterized these poems as non-Symbolist. However, Decadent many of them certainly are. The erotic theme is given much fuller rein here than earlier. So too is the exotic, particularly in the section "Cryptomeria." (Bryusov's brother later wrote that this title only *seems* exotic, being the name of a plant cultivated by their mother. This technique of exoticizing the everyday is typical of Bryusov's method.) The sonnet "Premonition" (see the appendix), especially in its revised form, exemplifies a theme which has attached itself—deservedly if somewhat disproportionately—to Bryusov's name: love as an amalgam of sensual pleasure, passion, and necrophilia, preferably in an exotic setting. At the same time he was engaged in formal experiments which, if not always artistically successful, yet pointed in new directions.

By the end of 1896 Bryusov was out with another collection, *Me eum esse,* which represents the apogee of his individualism. He called it his new poetry, and, writing earlier in the year, he noted with delight that "these poems are completely unlike *Chefs d'oeuvre,* as if someone else had written them." Indeed, in form they are more austere and perhaps technically better. But equally important is the total shift of thematic focus. *Me eum esse* is a book about poetry and the poet. Moved by his conception of Decadence and in particular by the writings of Poe, he now treated the world of reality as inconsequential. Proclaiming the superiority of art over all else, he withdrew into his world of icy perfection and "unearthly beauty."

However, this was not a permanent stance. Even before seeing the reviews of *Me eum esse*, Bryusov decided that it was time to retreat and take stock. Nearing twenty-three, he entered a major intellectual crisis. Throughout his various theoretical shifts and ponderings, of one thing he had remained fully convinced: the primary importance of the poet's personality. His was a truly Romantic conception of the poet. All poetry was for him lyric; to enjoy it was to communicate with the soul of the artist. However, this presented a problem: what if the artist's soul turned out to be not quite so rich as he thought? It was time to do something about his spiritual state. At the end of 1896 he promised himself a two-year period of reading only the great books—the Bible, Homer, Shakespeare—and writing only when he had something to say to the world. This moratorium was a tall order for Bryusov, but indeed, though he wrote during that time, he published little. In fact, he was busy enough: he progressed to his last year at Moscow University, he travelled to Germany, and he was married.

The poetic fruit of this period filled his third volume, *Tertia Vigilia* (1900), the first in which he appears as a mature poet. In the preface to this book he reiterates with new conviction his beliefs about the necessary freedom of art to express the individual soul of the poet. He himself has adopted some new themes. In *Tertia Vigilia* the theme of the city is developed, and not necessarily in its Baudelairean aspect. Nature makes its first appearance. And history, Bryusov's great love, informs a large section called "Favorites of the Ages." Here the forms are dramatic or lyric monologue, or address to figures ranging from Cassandra to Napoleon. In these works Bryusov's art has made a long stride.

By 1900 Bryusov was a full-fledged man of letters. He had made important contacts in Petersburg, he had published serious articles and research in *Russian Archive,* and he was an influential figure in the new publishing house Scorpion. (The names of both Scorpion and the journal *The Balance*—Libra—bore witness to the general Symbolist interest in the occult.)

Founded by the cultivated scion of a Moscow merchant family, Sergei Polyakov (translator of Knut Hamsun, Ibsen, and others), Scorpion for the next decade published the newest and best in Russian writing as well as European. Its publications were discriminating and handsomely turned out. Without Scorpion, the Russian Symbolist movement would be hard to imagine. For Bryusov it was a solid power base. In 1901 he and Polyakov initiated a series of miscellanies called *Northern Flowers,* which appeared irregularly until 1911. (The title was taken from a similar publication of Baron Delvig in the 1820s, to which Delvig's friend Pushkin had contributed.) The reincarnated version served as a prime vehicle for the Symbolists.

In 1903 Scorpion published Bryusov's *Urbi et orbi.* With this book he assumed the unquestioned position of Russia's leading poet. His art had reached its highest level. He was now truly in a position where his experiments, for example with rhythm and rhyme, could have the maximum impact on other, younger poets. He now set standards for all who followed him. His repertoire of genres and themes had expanded to its fullest. But exotica and especially erotica were still there, and so was the city as a lyric theme. His most striking achievement is the section "Ballads." Not ballads in any traditional sense, but lyric monologues in exotic frames, they are richly sound patterned and high in emotional tension. Many have called *Urbi et orbi* Bryusov's finest book, in the sense that his subsequent work, even including the splendid *Stephanos* (1906), was a continuation.

The year 1904 saw the beginning of another Scorpion enterprise, a journal called *The Balance,* of which Bryusov became *de facto* editor. The following six years were intense and often difficult. Many times Bryusov complained that he carried the journal's entire burden on his shoulders. There were periods when the strain, both personal and professional, among the all-star staff nearly tore the journal apart, and Bryusov acted the diplomatic peacemaker. There was a long period of violent polemic between *The Balance* and other Symbolist factions. During these years Bryusov turned out, besides his routine writing for the journal, a major historical novel, a collection of short fiction, two volumes of poetry, numerous substantial articles and a large body of translation.

Unfortunately, Bryusov's diary for these years breaks down. Fragmentary entries reflect the extreme turbulence of his personal life in 1904 and 1905, years of involvement with Nina Petrovskaya (see below), and his rather detached interest in the Revolution of 1905. They sketch his several journeys abroad but say almost nothing about *The Balance,* though his life's blood went into it. We turn to correspondence and archival records, where available, to flesh out this period. One thing that emerges clearly is the fact that Bryusov's interest in the Symbolist cause had appreciably cooled as early as 1906. Symbolism had changed and so had the literary atmosphere. It was no longer necessary to fight battles for the new art that had been largely won. In addition, the so-called second generation Symbolists, with their different interpretation of Symbolism, were essentially alien to him. Bryusov himself had changed, as is witnessed by his move, after the closing of *The Balance,* to *Russian Thought.* This was a literary-political-philosophical monthly published and edited by the economist and important Cadet party figure Peter Struve. By 1910 Bryusov was no longer interested in being avant garde. *Russian Thought* was far from dull, but its excitement was largely intellectual in nature. The journal carried an aura of very high-calibre respectability.

Bryusov remained with *Russian Thought* till the end of 1912. During the next five years he published more volumes of poetry, another collection of fiction, literary essays, theory and criticism, more translations. In 1913 the great hope of his career seemed about to be realized: a collected edition of his works in twenty-five volumes. The plan fell through with only eight volumes in print, owing to the liquidation of the publishing house Sirin.

From the outbreak of the war until May 1915 Bryusov was a war correspondent. At first full of fervor, after a few months he was totally disillusioned and ill besides. Back from this stint, he turned to various literary occupations. For a time one of his concerns was the poetry and culture of Armenia. At the request, prompted by Maxim Gorky, of the Moscow Armenian Committee, he edited and partially translated a collection of Armenian poetry, which came out in 1916. Taking a scientific attitude to everything on earth, as his wife said, he went on to produce a history of the Armenian people, earning him the special favor of Armenian scholars ever since.

If Bryusov was born a poet, as he believed, he was also a born administrator. For many years active in the Moscow Literary-Artistic Circle, he was its chairman from 1908. The Circle had been founded in 1898 by a group of prominent Muscovites including men like the art patron Prince Andrei Urusov, Prince Alexander Sumbatov-Yuzhin, the actor and director of the Maly Theater, and the sleek "Moscow Parisian," psychiatrist Nikolai Bazhenov, who regarded the new artists as objects of professional interest. Into this group a few rebels were allowed to infiltrate. Possibly through Bazhenov's interest, Bryusov was elected late in 1902 to the Circle's literary commission and was shortly appointed to a committee "for the organization of Tuesdays." These Tuesday evenings soon became events for all Moscow and beyond. Led at first by Konstantin Balmont and Bryusov, representatives of the new art read papers, defiantly recited their own poetry, and generally disported themselves with insolent self-assurance. Prominent lawyers, doctors, journalists, and their well-upholstered wives listened majestically and disapprovingly. The Tuesday evening discussion periods sometimes turned into scandalous proceedings which were duly reported in the Thursday papers. The novelist Boris Zaitsev recalled Andrei Bely challenging a member of the audience to a duel and being dragged away by Zaitsev's wife and Nikolai Berdyaev, the philosopher. The then budding poet Vladislav Khodasevich remembered how, to get into a session, he disguised his high-school status by wearing black pants. It seemed to him and others then that everything said was terribly significant and necessary. The fact that it turned out not to be so hardly diminished the Circle's importance during its twenty-year existence. Later the establishment grew in splendor: it continued to host meetings of various stripe, and it acquired an impressive library, gambling hall, and excellent dining facilities. As chairman, Bryusov ran the whole operation, down to the dining room, with tremendous skill and attention to detail. It was his last empire. When the Circle was closed after the Revolution, he was sufficiently powerful to obtain its library for his new base, the Literary Division of the Commissariat of Education. Nevertheless, his authority, as distinct from power, was not to be resurrected. For Bryusov there could be no return to the days of Scorpion, *The Balance,* and the Literary-Artistic Circle.

2

Remembering the balmy days of Symbolism, Vladislav Khodasevich wrote that the movement possessed a *genius loci*. People who breathed its air came to form a breed apart, forever marked with its sign. Their lives became inextricably intertwined with each other, and with their own writings, as well with those of others. "The writer cannot be separated from the man. Thus Symbolists also were tangled in a common net of personal and literary loves and hates," wrote Khodasevich. Symbolism was a method of living as well as of writing. Seemingly it called for an extra bit of something by way of temperament. Bryusov expounded this teaching and practiced it perhaps as consistently as most. Fire he had, but his personality lacked the quality of spontaneity and elemental abandon of either Balmont or Bely. Possibly because of this, he strove tirelessly to expand the limits of his experience beyond the rational. This drive provided a kind of divine fire of its own. By one means and another he sought to escape into the beyond: poetry, passion, spiritualism, magic, delirium, and later, morphine. Of these, the first two were closely blended.

For Bryusov, if a Symbolist's life *was* his poetry and vice versa, passion was the joining point. Thus relations with women were brought ostentatiously into his writings, and many if not all of these relationships themselves had literary models. For example, he wrote in his youth that he wanted to be the hero of a novel. In particular, he was drawn to Pechorin, the burnt-out Romantic protagonist of Lermontov's *Hero of Our Time.* There is often nothing very striking about a poet's early love poetry or its objects. Bryusov's early lyrics are sprinkled with dedications to various Talyas, Manyas, and Katyas. However, one of these early loves seems to have a certain importance. She was "Lyolya"—Elena Maslova. The romance lasted a short time (see the Diary, March 10 to May 20, 1893), and terminated in the heroine's death of smallpox. In his fictionalized autobiography *My Youth,* written in 1900, Elena Maslova appears as Nina Karina: twenty-five (contrasted to Bryusov's nineteen), far from pretty, with "lunatic eyes," already fading and resorting to powder and rouge. He had been snubbed by her younger sister, and "since in fact it was all the same to me with whom I fell in love—I simply needed some figure to write verses to and dream about—I immediately transferred my affections and fell in love with Nina." His "childish dream" of seduction came true easily. At that time, he notes, he was reading Baudelaire and Verlaine and had convinced himself that artificial beauty was better than natural. Moreover, Nina-Elena was soon to prove herself the perfect lover for a Decadent by dying. Necrophilia early became a theme of Bryusov's poetry. How genuine was his feeling for Elena? At the time, one gathers, he hardly knew; but seemingly it grew more important after her death. Diary entries (some unpublished) express intense grief, though in phrases suspiciously literary. She continued to appear in his poetry as late as 1916, and he used her surname as a literary pseudonym in his first publications. At the very least, she was a useful inspiration for a budding Decadent poet; she may have been more.

Some of Bryusov's other intrigues had greater impact than did Elena Maslova, both on his creative work and on his reputation. The best known of these is his link with Nina Petrovskaya. This was one of those relationships woven tightly into the Symbolist web. A young writer with entrée to Symbolist circles and a thoroughly Decadent personality, Nina Petrovskaya had an influence on literary life in Moscow for a few years beginning in 1903 disproportionate to her very slender talent. She was the wife of Sergei Krechetov-Sokolov, a minor Symbolist and publishing figure of some importance. She fell in love with Andrei Bely but lost him to Lyubov, wife of Alexander Blok. She then turned to Bryusov, first for help in her revenge against Bely, then as the focal point of a new emotional vortex. The Bely-Bryusov-Petrovskaya triangle was clearly a harrowing experience for all three. And it conformed admirably to the Symbolist doctrine that life and art should be one. A clear, unbiased account of the complicated affair is not to be had. But evidence of its literary impact abounds: Bely's poetry in 1903 and 1904, which reflects first his relations with Petrovskaya, then his enmity for Bryusov; Bryusov's collection of poetry *Stephanos* (1906), which records the romance; and most important his remarkable novel *The Fiery Angel*, laid in sixteenth-century Germany but portraying in its main characters the relationship of the three. There are also retrospective accounts: Vladislav Khodasevich's essay "The End of Renata" (Bryusov's heroine, who was burned as a witch); and Nina's own memoir, published in 1976, though only in excerpts. The latter is much kinder to Bryusov. Looked at from Bryusov's side, whatever its personal costs, this prolonged episode was extremely fruitful for his art. In a letter to Nina of June 1906, he wrote that his meeting with her had returned him to life as a poet. Having finished *Urbi et orbi*, he found himself empty. As he put it, he had pillaged his mine instead of extracting from it. His love with Nina had restored his powers, his mine was richer than before: it produced *Stephanos*. (The effect was not very prolonged, for in June 1906, he was again in a state of artistic and emotional exhaustion.)

The Fiery Angel had been conceived much earlier and was published in *The Balance* in 1907. Along with Bryusov's immense historical research it reflects his interest in black magic. As with anything else which caught his attention, he studied the subject thoroughly, reading deeply in occultism and perhaps taking his attraction still further. Aware of these researches, Bely accused Bryusov of carrying on "an extremely suspicious psychological experiment," namely, of attempting to hypnotize him. The duel in verse between the two in 1904 and 1905 took on the character of light versus darkness, with Bryusov willingly cast in the latter role. Bely's precarious psychological poise made him extremely vulnerable to the suggestion that he, the bearer of light, was threatened by a sinister, dark figure, i.e. Bryusov. Yet Bryusov was not merely playing games, if we can believe Nina Petrovskaya. (She reported to Bely that, after receiving Bely's poem "To an Old Enemy," Bryusov dreamed of a duel with rapiers, during which Bely pierced him through. He woke with a chest pain.) In February 1905, Bryusov challenged Bely to a duel, from which the latter hastily withdrew. A short time after, Nina pointed a revolver at Bryusov (or, according to Khodasevich, at Bely). The gun misfired, or was seized, and she never made another attempt. The dueling was apparently over.

The seven-year relationship between Bryusov and Nina followed a tortuous path, as witnessed in their unpublished correspondence. Finally, in 1911, Nina left Russia and Bryusov for good. Nevertheless, Khodasevich (a not disinterested observer) was almost certainly unfair to Bryusov when he concluded that, once Nina had provided the plot for *The Fiery Angel,* "it was tedious for him endlessly to relive the same chapters." Let down by Bryusov though she eventually was, her memoirs treat their relationship as the great event of her life, the tragedy which made life worth living. She pictures Bryusov as a man of profound spiritual depth. Her description is clearly meant to counter the view of him as a shallow manipulator, a stage manager of calculated effects, propagated by Khodasevich and Zinaida Gippius among others. To the question "What did Valery Bryusov see in me?" she answers: a kinship with the dark, secret side of his soul. "Desperation, a fatal yearning for a fantastically splendid past, readiness to hurl one's worthless existence into any bonfire . . . a thirst for ruin and death," in short, all that he needed for Renata, he found in Nina. But apparently he found much that he needed also in life. And Nina found her function, holding up before him his demonic image, forbidding his lapse into the character of a Moscow bourgeois concealed under the black cloak of the magus. It is part of Nina's image of him that he should put art above all else, including love. "For one splendid line on his future monument he would, without a second thought, cancel out the life dearest to him." Bitter as it is, such a remark contains its own kind of hero-worship. Nor was this her final judgment on him.

Shortly after Nina Petrovskaya's final departure from Moscow, Bryusov began paying his attentions to another beginning poet, Nadezhda Lvova. By a curious coincidence, Khodasevich was friend and confidant to Nadya as well as to Nina, and has written an account of the second affair as well. Much younger than Bryusov, Nadya Lvova apparently fell deeply in love with him. He became her mentor in poetry also. In 1913, when she published a small volume of verse called *An Old Fairy Tale,* Bryusov wrote a short foreword, praising her work, though in very sparing words. From some of these poems one may believe that she was preoccupied with death. Khodasevich reports that Bryusov was "systematically accustoming her to the thought of death, of suicide," and that he presented her with a revolver, the very Browning Nina had aimed earlier. The wonder is, perhaps, that she too did not point it at Bryusov. In fact, in 1913 she used it on herself. Was this another "extremely suspicious psychological experiment"? Did

Bryusov, who wrote continually on the theme of love and death, wish to experience death vicariously through a lover? Had the necrophilic image of Elena Maslova become faded? Earlier that year a curious small volume called *Poems to/by Nelli* (the Russian is ambiguous) appeared with an introductory sonnet by Bryusov. Nelli was his pet name for Nadya. The poems are written in the person of an elegant, worldly young woman recounting her amours. They have generally been regarded as Bryusov's, though hardly his best productions. Again, vicarious experience or psychological experiment? Or simply an unsuccessful poetic one?

Nadya's suicide affected Bryusov powerfully. He fled, first to Petersburg, where he saw Gippius, then to a sanatorium in Riga. Gippius writes that at that moment she saw in him a "real" man experiencing real remorse and perhaps real fear of death. However, to her regret this "real" Bryusov proved ephemeral. This tragedy climaxed an extremely turbulent and destructive period in his life. Nina had introduced him to morphine. In other ways he was near collapse. Nevertheless, Khodasevich relates with horror that Bryusov returned from Riga with new poetry, written in the sanatorium, celebrating a new love and repeating the refrain "Peace to the departed." Khodasevich obviously regarded this as characteristic callousness or worse. However, it may be seen as characteristic in another way. Repenting of his self-revelation to Gippius, Bryusov may have been demonstrating his "upward and onward" rule of life. This rule he applied, however brutally, in all situations, not least the personal and emotional.

Interestingly, Nadya Lvova emerges somewhat differently in Ilya Ehrenburg's memoir *People and Life 1891—*

1921. Before his departure from Russia in 1908, Ehrenburg had known her quite well in the underground movement. He notes that before her death Nadya had been translating the poems of Jules Laforgue, in one of which a young girl drowns herself for no known reason. Like Khodasevich, he pictures Nadya as a simple, bright, and capable girl. His chief point is the fact that her life had dimensions other than melancholy poetic feeling. "In the preface to the posthumous edition of her book I read: 'In Lvova's life there were no significant external events.' Dear Lord, how many events do there have to be in a person's life? At fifteen Nadya became an underground activist, at sixteen she was arrested, at nineteen she began to write poetry, at twenty-two she realized: 'I'm only a poetess'—and shot herself. I'd have said that was enough."

Bryusov's involvement and possible responsibility were recognized by everyone, beginning with his wife. She is said to have begged Khodasevich and others to arrange matters so that the newspapers would be discreet. Joanna Bryusova (or Eda, as Bryusov christened her) rarely appears in the dramatic episodes of his life. Yet she does appear in a more serene and tender strain of his poetry little remarked on and barely related to the erotic or Decadent themes. And it includes some of his loveliest. The tendency has been to regard her as the passive, faithful, neglected spouse. However, Eda seems to have been a spirited and intelligent woman. She came to the home of Bryusov's parents in 1897 as French tutor to the younger children. Valery, who lived in a separate part of the house with his father and usually brought a book to meals, caught her on one occasion with a rough copy of one of his poems, which she had rescued from the family kitchen. He began to notice her, and they were married the same year. In the preface to the 1933 edition of his *Selected Poems* she writes briefly of their courtship and includes a letter Bryusov wrote to one of his friends about his coming marriage. Clearly she had enough penetration into her husband's character to be ironically amused. How, after all, does a Decadent explain that he is about to wed a modest, intelligent, very un-Bohemian little French teacher and settle down to bourgeois domesticity at the age of twenty-three? She is described in rather unflattering terms: not beautiful, not too young, not too talented. The poet wants no George Sand to his Musset. However, "there is one great consideration before which the others are nothing—it is love, her love." He could hardly have been more correct. Zinaida Gippius characterizes her as the "eternal wife," remarkable only for her unremarkableness and for her willingness to wait for him as long as necessary. Quite possibly Gippius overlooked some qualities in a woman so different from herself. Joanna Bryusov's spirit, fortitude (and tolerance) were in fact essential to her husband's existence. Further, her influence on his posthumous reputation was of considerable importance. Except for the émigré memoirs, nothing of or about Bryusov was published for forty-one years after Bryusov's death which Eda did not in effect control. Her life from 1924 to 1965 was spent in editing his works, preserving and organizing his archive. She thought it unnecessary, except in the most sparing way, to present her version of their story.

"Eda" was the title of a Romantic poem by Baratynsky, in which the simple Finnish heroine is loved and ruined by a faithless Russian hussar. Bryusov and his bride-to-be read this poem in the early days of their courtship. But the pattern of their relationship, despite his many betrayals, was quite different. Nina Petrovskaya felt the pull exerted on him by Eda and domesticity, though she chose to see his retreats into homelife as lapses from his "greatness." Nearly every poem in the cycle "The Dear Truth" in *Tertia Vigilia* (1914 edition) is dedicated to Eda, as indeed are many poems throughout his work. Diary entries following their marriage and those describing two trips to the Crimea made with the entire Bryusov family prepare one for the themes associated with Eda in his poetry: tenderness, serenity, love of nature and of life. One is tempted to see her as a healthy, balancing influence. No doubt she was, but it is also possible that in 1897 Bryusov was ready for such an influence. His artistic crisis, dating from late 1896, has already been mentioned. The intention to bury himself in great books was coupled with another, seemingly contradictory one, to withdraw *into* everyday life. The Bryusov emerging in the diary of that time was a young man, Symbolist poet though he might be, who found considerable pleasure in the ordinary. At least for the time being.

After his early dash toward notoriety, Bryusov was content for a time with a more solid, graduated approach to the summits. During the later 1890s his circle of literary friendships and associations widened considerably. Only a few of these relationships bore the exotic character described by Khodasevich. The atmosphere was not yet dense enough to support them. That would come later.

3

In February of 1894, when Bryusov and his high-school friend Alexander Lang greeted their brainchild, the first volume of *Russian Symbolists,* the Moscow movement consisted practically of just those two. There were others, of course, but they had not yet become visible to one another. Bryusov's little book, with its optimistic title, shouted, "Here we are!" No reputable periodical might print their poetry, but at least these organs now recognized their existence, and they began to believe in it themselves. Almost immediately Bryusov started receiving verses from other hopeful Symbolists, and in June he was visited by two young Petersburg poets, Vladimir Gippius and Alexander Dobrolyubov. The latter's personality and poetry impressed him deeply.

Alexander Dobrolyubov was a consummate Decadent and, to Bryusov's mind, a remarkable poet with valuable ideas about poetry. Still a high-school student at the time of the Moscow visit, Dobrolyubov was subsequently expelled from St. Petersburg University for preaching suicide among the students. He then turned to religious asceticism, was for a time a novice in the Solovetsky Monastery in the far north of Russia, and still later formed a Christian anarchist sect, the Dobrolyubovians. Bryusov's favorite sister Nadya was at one time attracted to him and his teaching. Bryusov tried without much success to reclaim Dobrolyubov for poetry. However, the "holy wanderer" was at least as interesting to him as the poet. His lengthy diary descriptions of the visits of this renegade suggest his fascination with a nature capable of such extremes.

This kind of attraction was a frequent trait of Bryusov's friendships. Later in the same fruitful year, 1894, he became acquainted with another poet of elastic nature and occasionally bizarre behavior: Konstantin Balmont. A few years older than Bryusov, Balmont had already taken some steps as poet and had just discovered the new art. His reputation was to peak and decline before Bryusov's. At the time of their first friendship, he was translating Edgar Allan Poe and had become a thoroughgoing Decadent. The type of "elemental genius" suited Balmont temperamentally. He seemed to *live* the role of Poe and Baudelaire. With Bryusov he spent nights wandering through Moscow, drinking and reciting poetry. They talked a kind of Symbolist language which crops up in Bryusov's diary when he speaks of Balmont, as if in the attempt to recapture those intoxicated moments. Bryusov admitted to learning a good deal from Balmont. Years later, he credited him with revealing to him the secret of music in poetry. However, their friendship was spoiled early, perhaps by jealousy on Bryusov's part, but also by his sense of a tawdry element in Balmont's achievement. For Bryusov, disagreements about poetry and the poet's vocation came too close to the bone to admit of much quarrel.

The friendships with Dobrolyubov and Balmont evidence a double attraction in Bryusov's nature. He was drawn toward superior poetic talent and toward characters more capable of exotic experience than he. On the one hand, he eagerly sought out talented people like the young Ivan Konevskoy, whom he regarded as the hope of Russian poetry before his drowning in 1901. On the other hand, a key to a good deal in Bryusov's behavior and in his poetry is found in a yearning for what did not come naturally to him. Perhaps his was indeed, as Nina Petrovskaya would have it, a divided nature: the dark side, drawn toward the mystery of being and the universal chaos that was such an important theme in the poetry of Tyutchev—in a word, the poet—but hobbled always by the rational, hardworking, businesslike entrepreneur of literature. Or perhaps he only longed for a nature attuned to the deeper mysteries and sought vicarious experience of it. At any rate, his eye for special talent or unconventional character accounted for numerous relationships. The first stages of his long connection with Andrei Bely showed something of this pattern. "The most interesting man in Russia," as Bryusov called him, possessed that combination of dazzling talent and *bizarrerie* of personality which could captivate Bryusov until the subject somehow forfeited his esteem.

One protracted relationship in which other elements predominated was that with Zinaida Gippius and her husband Dmitri Merezhkovsky. When Bryusov began visiting them in Petersburg at the end of 1898, it was no doubt particularly the latter's established reputation which drew him. Before long, when literary life in Moscow became more lively—and profitable—the Merezhkovskys found it convenient to return the visits. The lively irony of Bryusov's accounts of them does not conceal his satisfaction with this connection. Merezhkovsky was pompous; Gippius was vain, sharp-tongued and demanding. Yet an aspiring poet and literary organizer would want the good will and good opinion of both. After the establishment of Scorpion, where Bryusov was a major influence, each side had something more to gain from the other. In the Merezhkovskys' eyes, Bryusov was a coming man and useful. For a short while in 1903, he served as secretary of their religious-philosophical journal *New Way*, but the alliance did not last long. Several years later a flirtation between the Petersburg pair and Bryusov on the subject of the Merezhkovskys' joining *The Balance* was aborted, with hard feelings on both sides. Over the years the personal relations of Gippius and Bryusov (personal relations with Merezhkovsky seemed hardly possible) were a sort of prolonged duel, mixed with flattery and a little coquetry. Basically, however, for both of them business was business, and their values were far apart. The fact that they chose opposite sides after the Revolution put an end to any connection at all and suppressed any favorable feelings which Gippius might ever have had toward her onetime colleague.

Obviously Bryusov was not a man who cultivated friendship for its own sake. His public stance was aloof, withdrawn, though in private he could be simple, kind enough, and very tactful. For younger poets he was a severe master. Some certainly saw him as a tyrant and later gleefully exposed the magician's bag of tricks. Khodasevich, school-chum of his younger brother and onetime hero-worshipper, afterward wrote of him with exquisite distaste tinged with disillusion. This would have been so, one feels, even without Bryusov's allegedly ruthless behavior to him in 1920. Khodasevich believed Bryusov capable of any betrayal if he thought it in the interest of poetry. Gippius pictured Bryusov as loving and desiring only fame; for Khodasevich, he loved only art. In a nature like Bryusov's these loves might well merge into one. There likely was room for little else.

4

Bryusov's life and career have been discussed in the literature rather more than his writings. This is probably inevitable because of his crucial personal role in modern Russian literary history. This emphasis is also justified by Bryusov's typically Symbolist belief that life and art are inseparable and by his care in preserving his own biographical records. He believed that the poet's importance lay especially in expressing the soul of his era. At least in his early years he felt acutely the contemporary quality of his own spirit and saw his function as embodying in his poetry the *fin de siècle* mood. His early, assiduous efforts at autobiography, beginning as they do in his mid-teens, may strike us by turns as amusingly adolescent and unbearably pompous. The youthful notebooks, each headed "My Life. Materials for My Biography," in fact contributed to a number of important published documents, of which the diary in this volume is one. And the insights gained from them are, as he intended, far from negligible for understanding his poetry.

Besides the diary, which was published posthumously, Bryusov printed a number of autobiographical writings during his lifetime. In the introduction to the fictionalized *My Youth,* he lays out his philosophy of autobiography in somewhat Rousseauian terms. The poet's duty is to transmit his soul. No man is too insignificant for his soul to be of interest to others. The poet is not one whose soul is essentially higher or worthier, but rather one who feels more acutely and is able to transmit his feelings. Furthermore, such an autobiographical account is interesting for the characterization of others and of the epoch. Working at *My Youth* the summer of 1900 on the seacoast at Revel in Estonia, Bryusov planned to publish it immediately as a description of a period of his life now finished. The account of a "contemporary soul" should be communicated immediately, for it might well lose its meaning after fifty years. As it stood, it would have been the perfect companion piece for *Tertia Vigilia,* published the same year. The work did not appear then, but there is no reason to disbelieve his thoughts on this subject of autobiography.

As his diary shows, Bryusov in his youth was keenly conscious of the passage of time and the pressure on the young artist to realize his talent. His enthusiasm for autobiography received a great stimulus in 1892 when he read with excitement the diary of Marie Bashkirtseva. This was a young Russian painter who lived and studied in Paris and whose talent was becoming recognized when she died at the age of twenty-four of consumption. Her diary, published in Paris in 1887, three years after her death, aroused great interest. It began to appear serially in the Russian journal *Northern Messenger* in 1892, where Bryusov read it. In Marie Bashkirtseva he found a spirit kindred to his in many respects: gifted, arrogant, fixed to an extraordinary degree on the goal of early fame, painfully anxious for fear of not reaching the goal in time. At fifteen she was writing: "To get all one can get out of life, and that quickly; . . . to be independent, so far as it be possible, of others; to possess power!—yes, power!—no matter by what means!—this is to be feared and respected; this is to be strong, and that is the height of human felicity. . . ." Reading this document at eighteen, Bryusov was inspired to write, "I must work! I must do something! . . . To work, life doesn't wait . . . . Forward! To victory!"

In some ways the Bryusov who emerges from the diary is very different from the one portrayed by contemporaries like Gippius, Khodasevich, and Bely, and by Marina Tsvetaeva, the young poet of genius who sought his notice and was painfully rebuffed. True, these accounts are colored to an extent by experiences with an older Bryusov. However, the difference is not entirely in that fact. The various portraits are not so much contradictory as complementary, but the autobiographical text understandably shows features missing from the others. For example, one important trait is Bryusov's capacity for self-irony. He clearly enjoyed posing, playing the role "Valery Bryusov." But he also enjoyed those who were not taken in, like the philosopher Nikolai Fyodorov or his school friend Pilsky, who, after the two had spent an evening parading their sophistication before each other, looked him in the eye, and the two laughed "like Cicero's augurers."

His tremendous capacity for work was well known in later years, and some, like Marina Tsvetaeva, used the poem in which he called inspiration his "faithful ox" to insist that he was all work and no holy fire. The exuberance of the lad who comes home from a carouse and writes eleven sonnets and two long poems is not to be discounted (regardless of exaggeration). But that he became a fine craftsman is unquestioned. That this took work he was at no pains to hide.

A perspective which one finds rarely outside his diary is that on Bryusov the student. His enthusiasm for the Latin poets and the great figures of Roman history played a part in both his poetic formation and his self-image. The pretentious comparison with Sulla and the trumpet flourishes in various passages are partly fun but partly a way of keeping his eye on the target of future greatness. Had he lived in 1830, his model would surely have been Napoleon. And finally, it can be a shock to remember that the arrogant author of *Chefs d'oeuvre* and *Me eum esse* trembled before his professors and crammed for exams.

Much that has been written about Bryusov in the last fifty years is colored by political views. He became a

Communist in 1919 after an earlier apolitical stance and served the cultural apparatus of the new regime until his death in 1924. For Soviet critics this redeems much in his writings, in themselves totally unconformable to Socialist Realism. For many others, and certainly for his contemporaries who went into emigration, it is a large deficiency. Opportunism is one of the milder names given to his actions. These facts have made difficult a real assessment of his literary quality; and, ironically, he might be said to have brought this difficulty on himself, with his insistence that art reveals the poet's soul.

Sometimes it is necessary to start over again in the effort to understand a writer whose image has been formed too quickly or under special circumstances. In the case of Bryusov, for any potential English-speaking audience, the problem is a different one: merely that of *starting*. In either case his diary is an excellent beginning, and the comments of his two brilliant (if not objective) contemporaries both add insights and demonstrate the controversial character of this poet who for an important decade gripped the imagination of Russia.

The Diary
of Valery Bryusov

1893

January 2. Welcome to thee, New Year! The last year of the second decade of my life, the last year in the gymnasium . . .[1] It's time! Get on with it, my friend!

Here is the program for this year: (1) Enter the literary arena. (2) One way or another break off with the K——ovs. (3) Graduate from the gymnasium brilliantly. (4) Take up an independent stance in the university. (5) Put all my convictions in order.

Incidentally, I'm about to make a try. Am sending translations from Verlaine to *News of Foreign Literature,* "Shadows" to *Artist,* and "Nikolai" to *Rebus.*[2] [None accepted.] [. . . .]

March 1. . . . Gymnasium exams are getting closer, and studies have become so revolting to me that I

THIS DIARY is an abridged translation of the version published in 1927 by Joanna Bryusova (*Dnevniki 1891–1900* [Moscow: M. and S. Sabashnikov, 1927]), which was itself substantially abridged. The complete text is in the manuscript division of the Lenin Library in Moscow and is not likely to be published in the near future. The present abridgement excludes the very fragmentary entries of the years 1891, 1892, and a few disconnected entries from 1905 to 1910. In making elisions elsewhere, I was guided by the wish to allow Bryusov's personality to emerge as clearly as possible and to retain information about the literary milieu and his relation to it. Ellipses in brackets are mine. All others are Bryusov's or his earlier editor's.

---

1. Bryusov graduated in 1893 from the Polivanov Gymnasium in Moscow with an excellent academic record, after making a very poor one from 1885 to 1889 in the Kreyman Gymnasium, along with a reputation for insubordination and disorderly conduct.
2. Periodicals are described in the Glossary of Proper Names.

can hardly touch a textbook. Am awaiting the next issues of *Foreign Literature* and *Review of the Picturesque*. Translating Mallarmé and getting ready to take the translation to an editor . . .

March 4. . . . Talent, even genius, by honest means earns only gradual success, if that. That's not enough! For me that's not enough. I must choose another way . . . Find a lodestar in the mist. And I see it: Decadence. Yes! Whatever one may say, whether it is false, or ridiculous, it is moving ahead, developing, and the future belongs to it, especially when it finds a worthy leader. And that leader will be I! Yes, *I!*

March 10. Yesterday was my nameday, and the K———ovs came to us. At first things were dragging, but after supper Elena Andreevna [Maslova] and I managed to be alone: at first we hid behind the map of Moscow and kissed, then we coolly went into another room . . . I recall that I babbled some kind of incoherent, decadent declaration—talked about the moon floating out of darkness, about a pagoda smiling in a stream, about a fantasy which burned out in the shape of a youthful dream. Nevertheless, she made a rendezvous with me for Friday and for Sunday. —Today, under the influence of all that, in a madly joyous mood, I personally carried to the office of *Russian Review* my Mallarmé translations. [Not published.]

March 22. What if I tried to write a treatise on spectral analysis couched in the language of Homer? I wouldn't have the words or expressions. The same thing if I try to express *fin de siècle* sensations in Pushkin's language. Yes, Symbolism is necessary!

March 26. [. . . .] Thinking back, I see that I have wielded great influence at school. Last spring I was engrossed in Spinoza; ethics turned up everywhere, and Yakovlev himself turned pantheist. In the fall I got interested in Merezhkovsky; everyone began reading [his] *Symbols*. Now I am—a Decadent. And so Satin, Kamensky, Yasyuninsky and lots of others are praising Symbolism. Bravo! [. . . .]

May 20. She's dead! Dead! She died of smallpox.[3]

June 14. I haven't recovered yet, though I'm gaining strength. I'm studying a lot and beginning to get back on the track. Am translating Verlaine with fair success and Ovid with much effort. I have decisively got the upper hand with Lang; he is now obedient. I think little about myself and my solitude and therefore am calm. . . . Am waiting for *Russian Review* to come out, so as to appear in the armor of a genuine poet. I'm thinking (among thousands of plans) about describing my love for Lyolya [Maslova] in a novella. My narrative poem on her death is going rather poorly. [. . . .]

3. Bryusov wrote in an unpublished section of the diary for May 7, "Lyolya [Elena Maslova] is ill (caught cold, perhaps, at our last meeting)." Subsequent unpublished diary entries show his intense preoccupation with her death. "She took with her everything. She was the only one who knew me, knew all my secrets. How hard to play a mere role before everyone. Always to be solitary. [. . . .] Terrible to think! When dying she was convinced that she caught cold coming to meet me . . . Dying, she was convinced that she was dying because of me." (See also the Introduction.)

1894

February 8. Yesterday I came down with a bad case of flu. Went to bed. A dose of antifibrin helped a lot, but Lang's letter helped much more: our volume *Symbolists* has been passed by the censor![4] *Eviva!* [*sic*] This is progress . . . [. . . .]

February 28. We're sending out *Symbolists* . . . I've written a marvellous poem, "The Violet," in the genre of Pushkin's "Last Clouds." [. . . .]

March 13. We were reviewed in detail in *New Times*. Of course, for me this is very flattering, all the more since they spoke of me as a gifted man. I feel like a real poet. [. . . .]

April 22. Sulla belonged to the same class of people as I. These are talented people *sans foi ni loi,* living only for their own pleasure. Very, very often they perform splendid deeds, but they are also capable of God knows what. Sulla was not annoyed by the reproaches of a citizen after formation of the dictatorship. But Sulla would in no way have considered it a crime to execute that citizen.

May 2. Today was the exam in Roman history . . . I did well—spoke about Herodian, about my tragedy, about poetry. [. . . .]

May 6. Studying fifteen hours a day, preparing for Church Slavic grammar . . . Am terribly busy, but at the same time am in superb form: I improvise a

---

4. Three volumes of *Russian Symbolists* [*Russkie Simvolisty*] appeared, two in 1894, one in 1895, all published in Moscow.

whole series of very charming verses; too bad there is no time to write them down. [. . . .]

May 11. Passed the exam . . . though not as brilliantly as Roman history. But no matter. [In English:] *Go ahead!*

They've torn me apart in *Universal Illustration.* [. . . .]

June 19. *Week of Symbolism.* . . . The past week was extremely valuable for my poetry. On Saturday there came to see me a little gymnasium student who turned out to be the Petersburg Symbolist Alexander Dobrolyubov. He dazzled me with his brilliant theory of literary schools, which alters all accepted views of the evolution of world literature. He unloaded a whole notebook of splendid poems by his comrade Vladimir Gippius. Dobrolyubov stayed till late Saturday evening, dined, etc. I was captivated. Analyzing his verses later with Lang, I found them weak. But on Monday Dobrolyubov came again, this time with Gippius, and I was again enthralled. Dobrolyubov came yet again, indulged in all kinds of oddities, took opium, in general was an arch-Symbolist. He subjected my verses to his talented criticism and revealed to me a good many things about poetry. It seemed as if everything was going well: Dobrolyubov was to write an article, the verses of both were to go into the second volume [of *Russian Symbolists*]; but, lo and behold, these two new Symbolists decided to look through the other poems prepared for that volume. As a result, they threw out more than half, and the rest they reworked till they were unrecognizable. On Saturday they brought them back to me. We disagreed and quarrelled. The alliance fell apart. Too bad! They're talented people.

June 20. As a matter of fact, Dobrolyubov was right in his criticism. Now, day and night, I'm rewriting verses . . . Funny—I was totally unable to charm him. Yet I know that he is no better than I am. All the same, I am attracted to him. —Those who have ears to hear, let them hear. [. . . .]

August 30. An interview with me came out in *News of the Day*.[5] Naturally this is far from distasteful. We move forward.

September 14. I was shown off like a trained animal to the members of Ivanov's household. I indulged in all the tricks of a trained beast—talked about Symbolism, recited poetry, waved my arms (a sign of originality) . . . I've written a Symbolist drama. Am writing a term paper on Solon and enjoying Greek authors. It's like meeting friends I haven't seen for a long time.

September 16. If there is one thing I am proud of, it's that I have never permitted myself to keep in my verses things I knew would please others, but which didn't please me.

September 28. I took part with Lang in the Society of Amateurs of Western Literature and met Balmont. After the drinking bout which ended the first ses-

5. A feuilleton entitled "Moscow Decadents" and signed "Arseny G.," August 29, 1894. In the interview Bryusov describes the new "school" in its variants, giving the impression that its members are already quite numerous. For example, he quotes a contributor to *Russian Symbolists* named Darov, who happens to be himself. Two days earlier the same paper had carried an interview with his coauthor Lang.

sion, we roamed about the streets, drunk, till 8:00 A.M. and swore eternal love . . . Yesterday I participated in Grot's seminar on psychology. I caught the whiff of philosophy, old philosophy I had forgotten. —I'm working on Solon, on an opera, on a drama, am finishing a lot of small things, etc.

October 11. Yesterday there was another meeting, and again Balmont and I roamed the streets till dawn in poetical dreams . . . Am writing Solon.

October 18. Have finished Solon. They've discussed it. It went quite decently. Balmont and others were at my place Thursday till about 2:00 A.M. Was terribly tired but somehow managed to discourse about poetry. [. . . .]

October 31. On Tuesday I was at Balmont's. Things went rather well. Returning home drunk at 3:00 A.M., I wrote eleven sonnets and two long poems. In general, I'm writing a lot. Am not going to classes at the university. [. . . .]

December 14. At the beginning of this notebook no one knew me, but now all the journals tear me to bits. Today *News of the Day* calmly mentioned "Bryusov," knowing that the name was familiar to their readers.

December 27. I am spending the end of 1894 quietly, mostly staying home, but working little. Went to see Balmont and wandered the streets with him all night. He spoke of purity of soul, of how sinful it is to drink wine and touch women. He spoke also of his *vita nuova*.

1895

February 1. [. . . .] Have seen Balmont several times. Most of our meetings have been semi-Decadent, but—alas—they've ended with a tavern and a "dive." I've come to see Balmont as he really is, and—again, alas!—he has lost much of his previous attractiveness. This is why I almost made fun of him Sunday at Kursinsky's . . . [. . . .]

March 21. *Chefs d'oeuvre* is recopied. Tomorrow I submit it to the censor. [. . . .]

May 7. I'm in a terrible situation. My Greek exam (the most important!), and I have an awful abscess, so that my eye is swollen shut. I'm struggling: you bear Caesar and his fortune![6]

June 7. . . . The last few days in Moscow [before going to the dacha] I had a plan for publishing *Chefs d'oeuvre* that involved pawning my gold watch, but the pawnshop wrecked that.[7] [. . . .]

July 1. I finished reading *The Count of Monte Cristo* with tears in my eyes, not because this novel reminded me of years gone by when I read it for the first time, but simply out of sympathy for the characters' fates. Stupid sentimentality about novels when one has none to spare for the events of life . . . [. . . .]

August 19. This evening Kursinsky came. We spent the whole time together, reciting poems without end . . . The influence of Tolstoy (whose children's

---

6. Plutarch *Caesar* 38.5; an indication of Bryusov's immersion in his classical studies.

7. *Chefs d'oeuvre* (Moscow, 1895; 2nd ed., 1896). Published at the author's expense.

tutor he is) shows in him more and more. I borrowed [Tolstoy's] *What I Believe* from him. He promised "The Kingdom of God is Within You" as well.

August 20. Still waiting for *Chefs d'oeuvre*. And because of that I can't get involved with anything else. Reading *What I Believe* and am moved.

August 30. I hear that Dobrolyubov has published a book of verse.[8] I'm terribly interested in seeing it. Am writing little and mostly prose. My *Chefs d'oeuvre* has produced—I have to admit—the very worst possible impression on my friends. They don't condemn it directly but keep quiet, which is even worse. My prestige with Friche has fallen. Only Lang (alas!) is faithful.

September 1. I've been so astonished by the polite silence of my friends about *Chefs d'oeuvre* that yesterday I ran to Kursinsky for support. He was not home yet, so I waited (he left Yasnaya Polyana only yesterday and got home today). Kursinsky is closer to me than the others.

September 8. The attack in the newspapers upset me terribly. I am carrying on a polemic as best I can (see *News of the Day*). However, an anonymous letter which came yesterday finished me off. I'm ruined. But it's consoling to think that "after sorrows come joys." What will they be this time?

September 11. . . . Today at the university when I volunteered to recite Aristophanes, everywhere I could hear them whispering and hissing, "Decadent, Decadent." Ah! so that's it! Watch out! Only the sincere

8. *Natura Naturans. Natura Naturata* (St. Petersburg, 1895).

sympathy of Samygin and Shulyatikov calmed me a bit. Ah, Kursinsky! I swear—you're cold. Watch out. [. . . .]

November 21. "Successes" continue to grow. After the favorable notice in *Russian Bulletin,* after the sympathetic interview in *News*—I'll see how my student-comrades treat me. The "ooh, Decadent" of not long ago has disappeared without a trace. "Yes," said N. N., according to Samygin, *"Chefs d'oeuvre* is a very remarkable book; there is a lot in it for the psychologist and the philosopher and student of pure esthetics."

December 13. Maybe it's a good thing I'm not being "recognized." If everyone were well disposed, I might be capable of falling to the level of people like Korinfsky and dancing to someone else's tune. [. . . .]

December 18. Balmont just dropped by, exultant, mad, Poe-like. Of course a great deal in his mood was affected, but nonetheless he cheered me up and distracted me. As if a moonbeam slipped through the clouds and scorched the waves with a brief kiss.[9]

December 20. I notice that the failure of *Chefs d'oeuvre* has knocked some self-confidence out of me, yet at one time it was completely genuine! Too bad.

December 27. The pitiful irony of fate. Now, when I am disillusioned with *Chefs d'oeuvre,* people begin to praise it—even Balmont! Balmont!

December 31. Verlaine is dead.

---

9. Bryusov is paraphrasing Balmont's lyric "Moonbeam."

1896

February 6. My future book *It Is I* will be a gigantic mockery of the whole human race. There won't be one sensible word in it—and of course it will find admirers. *Chefs d'oeuvre* is weak precisely because it is middle-of-the-road: too poetic for the critics and the public, and too simple for the Symbolists. Fool! I thought I was writing seriously!

February 27. Yesterday Balmont came by before his departure for Petersburg. O Lord, how untimely "fame" comes! Six months ago I'd have been ecstatic from half of the compliments he paid to me, but yesterday I felt "cold" disdain.

March 5. I have been feeling that to live as I live is impossible. Monotonous sameness, silence and longing. On Sunday I was in such despair that I couldn't even read Edgar Poe. Noise, family conversations, my relatives' stupidity—I put on my coat and decided to run away, despite my rheumatism . . .[10] As I was going out the door, I met Balmont. Then came a mad evening, people I didn't know, taverns, wine, arguments. I woke up . . . It was sordid, but I felt wafted over me the "azure of renewal." (Mr. Kursinsky's expression. See "Half-Shadows.")

March 6. Balmont was here today—we've become very close—and insisted that I read three studies of Maeterlinck appearing in No. 2 of *Northern Messenger*. I

---

10. Bryusov was bedridden and hospitalized with rheumatism for several weeks before this.

read them . . . Strange—all that Unseen Goodness, Inner Beauty, etc., produced on me the impression of *hidden* poetry.

April 7. Here I am in Petersburg. I've been running around, seeing the city, visiting theaters, etc. Saw Dobrolyubov. Alas! a ruin of the former Dobrolyubov, a meek, fawning youth. Life has trampled him, and I love him . . . But . . . he'll have no readers! However, Vladimir Gippius—there's a man fated to be victorious! He is proud and bold and self-assured. In a year he'll be read and in five he'll be a celebrity. All hail to him.

June 27. Little by little *Me eum esse* is getting written.[11] I'm delighted that these poems are totally unlike those in *Chefs d'oeuvre,* just as if someone else had written them . . .

July 4. Man is a strange and stupid creature. Yesterday I was reading [Dostoevsky's] *The Insulted and the Injured,* and suddenly I was overwhelmed by the maddest desire to take in a little orphan or a ward. Funny, crazy, but I began to walk back and forth in the room and imagine my whole conversation with her, where I would lodge her, what would transpire later, etc., etc. [. . . .]

July 26. I'm reading Turgenev.[12] Ah! Remarkable that the "I" of Turgenev's novels (even when the narration is in third person) is always an unimpor-

11. *Me eum esse* (Moscow, 1897).
12. Though his diary does not record it, Bryusov spent the summer of 1896 in Pyatigorsk, a Caucasian spa. From there by mail he put his sister Nadya through a reading course in Turgenev; hence his rereading of him and other novelists.

tant, ordinary type of person. Turgenev is totally helpless in the realm of psychology, and all of his more or less complex characters are delineated only through the eyes of another character. After Dostoevsky, Turgenev produces a sorry impression. What, for example, is "The Diary of a Superfluous Man" compared to (the second part of) *Notes from Underground?*

July 31. Have been reading Tolstoy. Here is the relationship among these three followers of Gogolian prose: Turgenev depicts the exterior, Dostoevsky analyzes the sick soul, Tolstoy the healthy one. If only these three were combined into one!

August 9. . . . . Turgenev describes the people who lived in his era; with his poetic intuition he guesses what so-and-so would say or do in such-and-such a situation—he guesses, but he doesn't know their souls. Tolstoy knows the souls of ordinary people, he says boldly what everyone knows, but he doesn't dare say what lies hidden in every soul. Dostoevsky knows the souls of exceptional people . . . [. . . .]

November 25. By chance I was at the university during the student disorders.[13] I got interested and asked questions, but in such detail that apparently they took me for a spy—*espion*—and asked a policeman to lock me with the rest of them in the riding academy, but

13. In November of 1896 the Moscow council of fraternities, a radical group, called a demonstration to commemorate the thirteen hundred victims trampled to death at Khodynka field near Moscow during the badly organized distribution of gifts following the coronation of Nicholas II. Bryusov was present on that occasion. The Moscow demonstration led to clashes with police and arrest of over seven hundred students.

I was rejected, and rather unceremoniously. I am printing *Me eum*.

November 26. "Now, several weeks before the publication of my most recent book of verses, I solemnly and seriously give my word to abstain from literary activity for two years. I would like to write nothing in that time and of all books to leave myself only three—the Bible, Homer, and Shakespeare. But even if this is impossible, I'll try to approach this ideal. I will read only what is great and write only in those moments when I have something to say to the whole world. I bid farewell to the noisy life of a journalistic warrior and the loud pretensions of a Symbolist poet. I will withdraw into life, submerge myself in its trifles, and permit my imagination, my pride, my ego to slumber. But this sleep will be only seeming. Thus a tiger closes its eyes, the better to watch its victim. And my quarry is already doomed to be mine. I am on my way. Trumpets, cease!"

December 11. I seem to be returning to life. The reasons for my "withdrawal" were many: both internal—exhaustion from the struggle, from reaction after finishing *Me eum esse,* new ideas—and external—scattering of all my friends, and suddenly much money [an inheritance] . . . For half a year I've done almost nothing for myself, nor for poetry, nor even for the university. Now I am being resurrected . . . I have set as the most immediate goal of my life a *History of the Lyric.* This work will occupy about three more years, if only I have free time, otherwise about five. [Begun but never completed.]

December 16. . . . Today I read the proofs of *Me eum* and the thirst for verses returned to me—but where is the "song-giving" source! Can I possibly be destined to live through what Fet did?[14] [. . . .] Muse, where are you! Alas, my former muse is dead, and the new one, which appeared to me among the cliffs of the Caucasus, has hidden her face and abandoned me, seeing how I offend against her best precepts . . .[15]

December 23. *Letter to Balmont in Paris.* —O, my brother! O, my brother! Today they brought me the first copy of *Me eum* . . . and suddenly I looked back on the past. Our wanderings in Sokolniki [Park]! Our cold arguments! My impassivity, oh, my impassivity! I did not expect such bitter mockery from life. Four months are erased from my life. Just as the Renaissance connects with the antique world, forgetting the Middle Ages, so the day of our separation was the eve of this day. They never happened, they don't exist—these fifteen long weeks, they did not happen!

1897

January 8. Petersburg. I roam the streets. There is a secret beauty in the way the churches disrupt the cold regularity of the boulevards . . . [. . . .] A collection of the lesser peculiarities of Petersburg: Petersburg women are more distinctive than Moscow women. Here there is a special style, a special chic,

14. The poet Fet, an important literary figure in midcentury, published a collection in 1863, then fell silent for twenty years, presumably owing to the hostile literary climate.

15. Bryusov traveled in the Caucasus during the summer of 1896 and worked on *Me eum esse.* He also was briefly infatuated with a sixteen-year-old girl to whom he dedicated several poems, noting his constant need of a Beatrice "in miniature."

which we don't have. The men, on the other hand, fall into the sorry type of street *viveur*. Debauchery in Petersburg is prettier to look at but more insolent. Nevsky Prospect is broad and long, and in the evening it is full to running over with street seductresses . . . Incidentally, the Nevsky is such an impressive artery that all the other streets are significant only in relation to it. There are other beautiful avenues—Liteyny, for example—and important commercial streets such as Gorokhovaya—or insolently self-assured ones like Voznesensky, but they are all secondary. Not like Moscow, where there is no sovereign, but several "aristocrat streets" reign—an oligarchic republic!

January 11. I went to see Sologub. Shcherbakov Lane turned out to be in the slums of Petersburg, located near the center. And No. 7 turned out to be a dirty heap with a stinking courtyard. To get to apartment eighteen I had to climb a narrow, slop-covered stair, and at last, at the very top, I read on the door: "Midwife Teternikova."

I hesitated: should I ring or not? At last I did. The apartment had two rooms; a female of uncertain age opened the door—"My sister," said Sologub. He himself has gotten balder, older. We chatted for about half an hour, rather formally. The chief thing I wanted I did not find out: whether Dobrolyubov received the fifty rubles he asked me for and which I sent from Pyatigorsk. If he received them, why didn't he publish anything? (After all, he wanted the money for "Some Observations.") But if my remittance didn't reach him, what must Dobrolyubov think of me! Tormented by this thought, I filed an inquiry at the post office.

January 24. [Moscow.] An answer came from the Petersburg post office. The remittance of fifty rubles was delivered to and signed for by A. Dobrolyubov. So he got the money. Well, so what! It doesn't keep him from being a splendid poet and a fine person.

February 6. Again, the dismal, colorless life. The history of the lyric, the Church Fathers, the Bible—that's all, unless you add tutoring my sisters and card playing with my father. Not much.

February 8. My voluntary isolation subjects me to a severe trial. Have I enough spiritual strength to preserve my aspiration amid the petty vulgarity of the life which surrounds me? Have I perceived my path clearly enough to follow it firmly amid gossip about money and conversations about women, amidst cards and carousal, alone in the whirlpool? My bright star! Stay pure and blessed. Do not fade . . .

March 11. Life is rather bitter just now. Little faith in myself, no goals, the past dark. Unpleasant clashes at the university. Guerrier said: "I've seen your new book. Perhaps that is enough to call yourself a poet, but it is not enough to make you a historian . . ."

March 15. What am I working on now? Immediate tasks: the foreword to *History of the Russian Lyric.* —A paper for Guerrier on Rousseau. A paper for Klyuchevsky (required, alas!). My symbolist drama. A long poem on Rousseau. A novel: *This Is A Story* . . . a story about Elena. —Translation of the Aeneid. —A little poem about Moscow. —A monograph, "Nero." —"Legion and Phalanx." Planned: a drama, "Marina

Mniszek," "Atlantis," and a translation of Maeterlinck's *Les Trésors*. A story, "The Exiled Women." In the future: a history of Roman literature. A history of the emperors. A history of Scholasticism. A public lecture on Rimbaud.

Reading now: Weber, Maeterlinck, the Bible, Sumarokov. Must read: Kant, Novalis, Boileau.

March 17. Writing? Writing isn't hard. I could write many novels and dramas in six months. But it is *necessary, essential,* to have something to write about. A poet must be reborn, he must meet at the crossroads an angel who will pierce his breast with a sword and place there, instead of his heart, a burning coal. Until that happens, you must drag yourself mutely through the "wild desert . . ."[16]

16. Paraphrase of Pushkin's poem "The Prophet," with small variation: "wild" for "sombre desert." The whole text, an important statement of the Romantic concept of the poet, reads as follows (line division mine):

Tormented by spiritual thirst / I dragged myself through a somber desert. / And a six-winged seraph / appeared to me at the crossing of the ways. / He touched my eyes with fingers / light as a dream: / and my prophetic eyes opened / like those of a frightened eagle. / He touched my ears / and they were filled with noise and ringing: / and I heard the shuddering of the heavens, / and the flight of the angels in the heights, / and the movements of the beasts of the sea under the waters, / and the sound of the vine growing in the valley. / He bent down to my mouth / and tore out my tongue, / sinful, deceitful, and given to idle talk; / and with his right hand steeped in blood / he inserted the forked tongue of a wise serpent / into my benumbed mouth. / He clove my breast with a sword, / and plucked out my quivering heart, / and thrust a coal of live fire / into my gaping breast. / Like a corpse I lay in the desert. / And the voice of God called out to me: / "Arise, O prophet, see and hear, / be filled with my will, / go forth over land and sea, / and set the hearts of men on fire with your Word." (Dmitri Obolensky, trans., *The Heritage of Russian Verse* [Bloomington, Indiana: Indiana University Press, 1976])

October 2. Petersburg. The weeks before the wedding are not recorded.[17] This is because they were weeks of happiness. And how can I write now if I can describe my condition with only one word, bliss? I'm almost ashamed to make such a confession, but what can I do, that's the way it is. Is this possibly the "intoxication" about which the old poets wrote so much? —No! No! —For so long I sought that closeness with another soul, that total merging of two beings. I was born for just such endless love, for endless tenderness. I have come into my native sphere—I was destined to know bliss.

To say, "I am happy" is to say a great deal. Do many dare say these words, to say "I am happy" in the present tense? In memory of these days I will not dare to condemn anything in the future. "Even if I am destined for a moment of repentance . . ."

October 23. Moscow. Peaceful life from day to day . . . I'm very busy with philosophy, and am reading with Eda [his wife]. Also writing verse. *Et vraiment je ne veux d'autre paradis.*

Kant, whom we are studying at the university, has totally absorbed me. Leibniz, whom I am studying for the seminar, gives much for the soul. Perhaps before *Corona* [*Tertia Vigilia*] and before the first volume of *History of the Lyric,* I will write *Philosophical Essays.* (Contents: I. Leibniz. II. Edgar Poe. III. Maeterlinck. IV. Idealism. V. The basis of all metaphysic. VI. Love [Two]. VII. Christianity.)

November 19. Balmont has come, he whom I so waited and longed for. —He is wearing a double necktie and his hair is so carefully cut . . .

17. Bryusov married Joanna Runt on September 28, 1897.

> La luna llena . . . A full moon . . .
> Inez is pale, kisses like a gitana.
> Te amo . . . amo . . . Stillness again . . .
> But the fixed gaze of Don Juan is grim.
> [BALMONT, "DON JUAN"]

We sat together in the [restaurant] Rossia. He recited, I barely listened. It seemed as if the time two years ago had returned, as if I were the former, self-assured poet . . . When I began to recite my verses, I was ashamed. Not of the verses—they are good—but of there being so few—two timid pieces—when he was reciting to me fragments of long poems boldly conceived, the beginnings of long narratives. For him life is more vivid than formerly, but mine is growing dim.

"I've come to love the fierce amusements / Of acrobats' flights, combat of bulls, / Arenas where boas twist, / And maidenhood, led into alcoves . . ." And this is closed to me now. And yet, the third line was borrowed from me, and because of this Balmont wanted to replace it with "And the howling of wolves escaping from encirclement."

November 21. We [Balmont and Bryusov] separated, not coldly but gloomily . . .

I wrote to Balmont today that I would be alone this evening. He came. I think he wanted to take revenge on me. He had so longed to see me, had created such a picture of me in his imagination. He wrote in his letters that I was the only person he needed in Russia. And of course the original isn't up to the dream! And besides, much that Balmont is seeking I will never accept. I have also changed in this year but changed not in the way he would have liked, and perhaps, alas, in a way he doesn't understand. —He wanted revenge; he mocked wickedly at everything I said.

We talked of Christ. Balmont called him a lackey, a philosopher for beggars . . . But is a conversation carried on in words? There is a dialogue of souls. And much was said. I felt like crying. When we parted, Balmont half apologized: "Don't be angry." [. . . .]

End of November. We were mistaken. We met again and the flame of love again quivered between us.

Balmont stopped by and didn't find me but left a note. I went to see him. There were many guests. Under cover of general conversational noise we managed to be alone, even to steal away by ourselves . . . [. . . .]

Another time Balmont came early in the morning, after a sleepless night; he woke me. We left the house quickly, roamed the streets, dropped into a bookstore, went to his place then to [Mirra] Lokhvitskaya's. It was a complete resurrection of the past. We rejoiced like children, laughing at everything. [. . . .]

However, we parted more coldly than I had expected. Perhaps he was offended by my negative remarks about Lokhvitskaya, who struck me as a rather untalented woman. Why does she have such a big mouth? And then she had to go and say to me: "I'm used to people diverting me." I answered: "Then we have nothing to say to each other." However, her most recent poems are good.

December 9. Obleukhov brought from Rozanov his *Legend* [*of the Grand Inquisitor*] with the inscription, "To the author of *Me eum* with the hope of a personal acquaintance . . ." [. . . .]

1898

January 18. [. . . .] The most important event of these days has been the appearance of Count Tolstoy's article on art.[18] Tolstoy's ideas so coincide with mine that at first I was in despair and wanted to write "letters to the editor," to protest. Now I've calmed down and contented myself with a letter to Tolstoy himself.[19] [. . . .]

January 29. I'm still not going out [after a bout of pleurisy]. Am leading the "quiet" life of a family man, reading French novels aloud to my wife, on Sundays playing whist and on the side writing my *Literary Essays*. [. . . .] Study of philosophy somehow kills off poetry. Poetry demands a certain naiveté of thought. The mind seduced by metaphysical refinements rejects the inexactness of poetic language.

Had a letter from Balmont. [. . . .]

February 11. I went out today for the first time after nearly two months' confinement. The fresh air intoxicated me; my head spun.

---

18. Tolstoy's *What Is Art?* [*Čto takoe iskusstvo?*] appeared first in excerpts in the journal *Problems of Philosophy and Psychology* 40, no. 5 (1897), and 41, no. 1 (1898).

19. On January 20, 1898, Bryusov wrote a letter to Tolstoy in which he expressed surprise that Tolstoy had not named him as a predecessor because of the ideas on art as communication expressed in his preface to *Chefs d'oeuvre*. His request that Tolstoy acknowledge him in print was, not surprisingly, ignored. Moreover, in a variant of his work, published only much later, Tolstoy took note of Bryusov and *Chefs d'oeuvre* without naming either. He quoted Bryusov's one line poem, "O cover your pale legs," as an example of nonsense being published "even in Moscow" by those who were either charlatans or mentally ill.

February 12. "Zola condemned." At one time I loved France and the French generally; after that Dreyfus affair and the condemnation of Zola, I despise and curse them. And my Verlaine was no Frenchman. [. . . .]

End of March. Two whole weeks wasted. I had to finish up at the university, to write for Guerrier, for Vinogradov, for Klyuchevsky—about the Constituent Assembly, and the "Lex Salica" and the travels of Olearius . . . Each paper was written in one night, and probably they don't rate very high marks . . . [. . . .]

April 3. Moved to Tsvetnoy Boulevard.[20] I'm living again with "the family." Am relaxing. Have given myself permission to do nothing. I play cards, I tell Nadya all about the Arabs and the Carolingians . . . Am looking forward to the Crimea.

April 9. I must go forward! I must conquer! Could all these proud beginnings, these plans, this work, this ceaseless work of many years possibly come to nothing? My youth was the youth of a genius. I so lived and acted that only great deeds can justify my behavior. They must occur, or I will be ridiculous. To lay the foundation for a temple and build an ordinary hotel! I must go forward, I have taken on myself that obligation. [. . . .]

April 15. Yalta. From the window there is a view of the sea; to the left is Massandra. Under the win-

---

20. The young Bryusovs lived in the rooming house Toulon from their wedding until April 1898, when they returned to an apartment in the family home on Tsvetnoy Boulevard.

dow the sea roars, foams, runs up on the wet rocks . . . In the distance all is silver; tiny ships out there, frozen, immobile. A half-gray sky. I will teach myself to love nature, and the sky, and the green sea, and the shore with its motionless cypresses. I came not to curse but to love. Shall I not come to cherish the white gulls, the wet rocks, the ugly dolphins in the waves! Under the window the sea roars, runs, foams . . .

April 19. Yalta. Five days of life with nature. The sea is now clear, calm, with dolphins, with gulls, and now foaming, roughened by an uneven wind which hurls it on the shoreline rocks; waterfalls shattered into spray even before falling, hanging like flying white dust over the abyss; and torrents, where it is wonderful to sit on jutting ledges amidst the roar of the water from above and below, drowning the voice. Everywhere is that wall of mountains, girding Yalta in a semicircle, with lines of snow in the high valleys, with black pines lower down, and covered with charming little houses on the lower slopes . . . Marvellous! Parks with magnolias, oleanders, myrtles, laurels, almond and olive groves, cypress alleys, multicolored foliage, the marble of columns wound with ivy . . . A fabulous land! Tauris![21] One believes the traditions, believes the paintings, and believes that all this is reality, that there is a charm in nature.

April 22. Alupka. I'm doing everything that befits a tourist and lover of the beauty of meridional lands: I listen to the sea, scramble on the rocks, look at various ruins. It won't be my fault if even now I will be unable to "fall in love" with nature. I've written "Pic-

21. From the ancient Greek name for the Crimea, frequently used in Russian poetry.

tures of the Crimea," four poems composed with every appropriate amenity.

April 23. Yesterday we climbed up Ai-Petri. Father stayed at the foot, but Eda and I tried to climb higher. We had to scramble up what was almost a sheer cliff, hanging on to tufts of grass, prickly bushes and loose rocks. Sometimes we simply crawled along a smooth stony slope. This way we got up to the second plateau, which is surrounded on all sides by cliffs. The path went no further . . .

The sea creates a strange impression under the full moon. The waves toss and beat as if struggling with some mysterious power. They form unexpected whirlpools, and the sea swirls and surges forward, then breaks and recedes. The waves rise high, high, and then fall back. And the moonlight shatters on the waves, curves about now like thick snakes, now like tiny bent wires. The moon looks down from a cloudless sky, white, regnant. In the park is a bench with the inscription: "Farewell, cozy bench, / Farewell, perhaps, forever, / But this charming nook / Will be forgotten never." All around there are rather ordinary trees, small cliffs, a stream nearby—nothing remarkable. How typical that some visitor from the north should turn up and prefer this nook, reminiscent of corners in gardens around Moscow, to all the splendid vistas of sea, massive crags, and roaring cascades. [. . . .]

May 8. "Blessed is he who in youth was young." This line from Pushkin that has almost become common coin says a lot to me. I was not young in youth, I experienced all the tortures of a divided soul. From my earliest years, I dared not give in to feelings. I spoke to many about love but for a long time dared not love. Two years ago, travelling in the Crimea, I couldn't make up my mind to enjoy nature without thinking. I was the slave of preconceptions and self-set goals . . . Oh, it took a great deal of struggling to understand that highest of all is one's own soul. And here, conquering everything that held me in thrall for a period of years, I am achieving both simplicity and sincerity, I am yielding to feeling, I am young . . .

"The ways of perfection are endless, / O, preserve each instant of being . . ." I shall follow this New Testament. [. . . .]

May 25. Our last week in the South is coming to an end. I clearly realize that it is time to go back, to my studies, to "meditations." Doing nothing and constant "admiring" of the pictures of nature have worn me out. Again you look, again you say, "How splendid," and search for proper epithets and comparisons, but the soul remains unmoved. However, I believe that the impressions also sink into the soul. May they be seeds which will develop into fragrant flowers![22]

June 9. [Moscow.] We abandoned the South too quickly, too soon . . . As always, as soon as we leave something, we feel the loss. How bitter and how painful. Why am I here in the vulgar surroundings of Moscow life and not there, where there are still the "incessant roaring" of the sea and the "coevals of the ages"—the cliffs? [. . . .]

June 14. Ostankino. We're in Ostankino, have rented a room from a general's widow named

22. See the section "By the Sea" in *Tertia Vigilia,* called "Pictures of the Crimea and the Sea" in the first edition.

Malevskaya. We're being very good and speaking in whispers so as not to disturb the landlords. I am opening my notebook and going to work.

Received my certificate of credit for eight semesters and was glad to get it. My last written work was done so badly, so sloppily, that I really deserved "no credit."

June 30. Peaceful existence. In the morning, studies; after a swim and dinner, come rest, algebra with my wife, sometimes berry picking, and finally, in the evening, tea with the whole family. Ah, I have long been savoring this peaceful life. Now at times I feel like screaming, "Go to hell, all of you!" But restrain yourself, my friend. I want to finish the article on art, and then I'll see. Am reading little and writing almost no poetry.

Two weeks on a vegetarian diet.

Went to see Samygin twice, the only person who enlivens my soul. Had a desperate letter from Balmont. "My friend! What darkness around, I am walking on red-hot steps . . ." I don't know whether I can find words to answer him. "My voice is losing nuances, / Nuances of dreaming words." [. . . .]

July 17. A letter from Dobrolyubov . . . Oh, so many strange and mad and improbable memories. Like a wild dream, suddenly coming to mind, and understood for the first time though I had had it long ago . . .

Alexander Dobrolyubov! Once I loved him. What can I find to say to him, the present "I"? Balmont and Dobrolyubov were for me in the past two ideals. I have changed since then; yes, I am different! But in their presence I don't dare be different, and I don't know how to be what I was. I'm powerless in their presence. And in my soul arises the question: what if that former "I" was better, higher? Woe is me! [. . . .]

July 28. Dobrolyubov is staying with me, I want to report in detail the two days which we have spent here in Ostankino together.

Returning to Moscow after visiting Samygin, we learned that Dobrolyubov had stopped by and that he was going to Ostankino. We rushed out there. He arrived shortly in a cab. A sore foot kept him from walking. He was wearing peasant dress: a coarse caftan, red shirt, heavy boots, a knapsack on his back and staff in hand. His face has greatly changed. I remember his face very well. There were (formerly) the childish features, the pale, pale face—and burning black eyes, sometimes looking off somewhere, as if into the beyond. Now his features have coarsened; he has a little beard all around his face, and there is something Russian in his face. His eyes have become more pensive, more assured, though it is in them that the past also has been preserved. His thick, black hair remains as before, now from time to time reflecting crimson from his shirt.

But how his habits and ways have changed! At one time he was as if from another world, clumsy, immensely self-assured because immensely shy . . . Now he has become simple, he can talk with anyone. He was able to say something to my little brother and my sisters and even to Mama. And everyone involuntarily smiled happily at his words. Even the animals went to him trustfully, to be petted.

He came from Pudozh. Last winter he went to Olonets province "above all to break with the whole past," as he said himself. He lived there all winter, hiked to Finland, walked on the ice of Lake Onega, went bear hunting. While living there he took the opportunity to collect folk songs, tales, charms, and laments. He knows a great many of them by heart, totally unknown ones, not recorded by anyone. He had written a few of them down, for example, what he called the "Russian Boccaccio"—stories about priests. He also came by a manuscript "Conversation about the Soul." And he gathered the "precepts" of Kozakov, a folk satirist, who recites them at weddings.

In the first hour of our meeting, before finding a subject for conversation, while talking rather fitfully, Dobrolyubov told me that he now has "found faith," that he has become different, and that the past weighs on him, that he condemns it terribly. But I will relate what I know of his life.

According to his account, in adolescence he was frightfully shy. When he was about twelve, he dared not look at women. Sitting at the same table with governesses, he covered his eyes with his hand. But already in those days he had dedicated himself to art and wanted to achieve everything. Once he was astounded to find that he was a very poor observer, that, for example, after talking with a person he didn't remember the color of his eyes, etc. Then he began to train himself. He would go up to the window of a store and then, coming away, write down every detail of what he had seen. He would write down a conversation in the streetcar, describe the view from a window—and these experiments covered hundreds of sheets of paper. His first things he often wrote in French. He began to study twelfth-century French literature with his teacher, and was still imitating those models. But, always shy, he couldn't bring himself to recite these verses to anyone.

By his account, Vladimir Gippius had a very strong influence on him. Apparently they became close while still boys. Gippius overcame the shyness and forced him to recite his verses. Moved by a sort of bitterness, Dobrolyubov painted Gippius as his evil genius. "He taught me to see everything bad," said he. "I would read poets, for instance you. I wanted to enjoy their merits, but Gippius hurried to point out to me their flaws. Often he changed my good opinion of someone to a bad one."

Under Gippius's influence, Dobrolyubov became what he was when I first knew him, the Symbolist Dobrolyubov. But his outstanding trait is that in everything he goes all the way. And here too he went all the way. Without doubt he is the most talented and most original of us, of all the new poets. But in his convictions he has also gone all the way. It would have been senseless to have called him a materialist. He was not that at all. But he recognized only this three-dimensional world, believed in no life beyond, did not distinguish good from bad, but only distinguished the image from the vulgar idea, the artist's creation from his thoughts. So he lived this way, as an artist, worshipping art as a holy shrine. For example, he held then that in the future there would be no science. People would come to the sea and compose a song about the sea; they would come to the mountains and compose a song about the mountains. In place of science, there would be a very detailed song . . . And along with this worship of art, he told himself that, if there is only this life, then nothing is forbidden, and he permitted himself everything. "I will tell certain of my sins to no one, for I am afraid that such a confession might lead them into temptation. And I am sure that others you could not even imagine, not even conceive of."

The book which he published contains some things that are utterly childish. Later he wrote down thoughts that were greater. That year when I was in the Caucasus, he wanted to print them. The manuscript was at the printer's, already being set in type. But at that time the rift had already begun in him. He struggled for a long time. Finally he decided that there was no one to print it for, that it was destined for too few . . . He threw over publication and left Petersburg.

Here something bitter happened. All of his manuscripts were lost at the printer. Many poems and prose fragments and maxims perished. In vain he demanded them back, nothing could be found. In bitterness and indignation he burned everything that remained or was salvaged. Soon after that, he returned to writing but did not want to reconstruct the past. Instead he wrote many new things with redoubled strength . . . Again he produced many poems and fragments.

But the rift was deep in his soul. He tried to ignore it. He described the most painful states of mind, all the while pretending the rift was not there. But at the same time he was withdrawing both from books and from his former acquaintances; with some like Gippius he quarreled several times. And then suddenly came the radical change. At first he came to believe in another world, as he had believed also in a temporal one. And this belief lasted for some time. Later he understood everything, as if all at once. During the very first days after this conversion, he was writing. But later he fell silent, stopped writing because his heart was occupied with other things.

I cannot say just where this change occurred, in Petersburg or in the Olonets province. But, now too, having found faith, he does not stop but is going all the way. His decision is firm. He is giving away all his property, dividing it among friends and enemies. Then he will go into a monastery for a year, probably at the Solovetsky. After that he will withdraw for several years into complete solitude, and then perhaps he'll teach, or perhaps simply write everything down so that people will learn of it after his death.

"How one can fail to understand oneself!" said he. "Several months before the conversion, I entered into a certain political conspiracy . . ." Their object was to transform Russia in the folk spirit, in lesser things such as clothing but also in essentials—thus to return to the folk their songs, which they are forgetting. But now he understands that all that is unimportant.

He made this journey from Pudozh to Moscow in order to see and to think. For most of the journey he was silent. He walked through the woods where gnats tortured him, where he might even have encountered bears; and he sang and made up songs so that no bear could come near him. The peasants received him hospitably. They begged him to recite charms or make the sign of the cross over the cattle. Near Beloozero his foot began to give him trouble, and he had a fever. He lay sick at the village teacher's. He had to continue his journey on wheels . . .

I don't want to set forth Dobrolyubov's teaching here. He can do that better than I. And if he doesn't, it doesn't matter.[23] But in his teaching he managed to be as original as in everything else. He hasn't given in, like the rest of us. [. . . .]

Dobrolyubov stayed with us two days and two nights. At first we talked a great deal. Then everything had been said. Arguing was useless, because he had thought every-

23. Dobrolyubov's teachings were published by friends in 1905 under the title *From an Invisible Book* [*Iz knigi nevidimoj*].

thing out. We would sit in silence for long minutes, but this didn't discomfit him. Sometimes we would talk . . . I would say something, he would be still for a moment and then answer, and after a long pause I would respond.

Eda and my sister Nadya were utterly enthralled . . . They looked at him as if he were a prophet and were ready to worship him. Mama secretly made fun of him; besides he is a vegetarian.[24] But how he has managed to transform himself! He, as he used to be! How graciously he now speaks with everyone! How he bows from the waist after dinner and thanks the "lady of the house."

We spoke of poetry. I recited some of my verses. On this matter, too, he has changed. There were none of the former sharp, murderous strictures. He pointed out what was good, but that was all. In general, he keeps a close watch on himself. [. . . .]

Later on, he recited some folk songs for me. He knew how to choose them, and he recited so well that they were simply captivating. Too bad he couldn't remember the one about horses . . . "Under him they writhe like snakes . . ." Finally, he also recited some of his own poems. He warned me that this was the past and it doesn't interest him now. But I noticed nonetheless that he has not been able to vanquish the artist in his soul completely. It was in the reciting of poetry that the old Dobrolyubov was alive . . .

. . . Dobrolyubov said to me: "The past was necessary. I had to find out the whole measure of sin. My preoccupation with poetry was not wasted either.

---

24. Bryusov's mother, of working-class background, was one of the young women of the early 1870s who cut their hair, took off their baptismal crosses, and went in for education and personal freedom. She did not greatly temper her ideas in later years.

Perhaps it served a purpose in that I later composed two or three airs."

July 31. The meeting with Dobrolyubov was a breath of something new; it enlivened, resurrected my soul. Oh, it's very hard on my spirit to be, if not entirely alone, at least not to know people spiritually higher than myself. And even the best of my friends, like Samygin, pull me downward. Now the words of Dobrolyubov have suddenly fanned the faintly flickering fires. Today I have reread my book on art, and all its impotence revealed itself to me.[25] To work, once again from the beginning! [. . . .]

August 4. Yesterday Dobrolyubov left. I saw him three times more. Two meetings in Moscow weakened the impression he made. He spoke of his past self, told me some uninteresting and even unattractive incidents in his life, and told them with apparent relish. He would often reiterate that he was Antichrist and cited prophecies to support it. He had written, against his vow ("in a moment of confusion," in his words), a prosaic poem about the revealed truth, which I didn't like.

But yesterday when he came back to Ostankino to say good-bye, he was fine once again. And he found something interesting from his past to tell. He related his theory of heredity. The wills of dead ancestors—he formerly supposed—remain external to us, and we know them as nature. The most ancient wills are the cliffs and rocks; wills from more recent aeons come to us as plants;

---

25. *About Art* [*O iskusstve*] (Moscow, 1899). This booklet contained the ideas which Bryusov was mulling at the time Tolstoy's *What Is Art?* appeared. In his preface he points out the similarities and differences between his ideas and Tolstoy's. (See also note 19.)

and the most recent, as animals. And our bodies also are the wills of former beings. Our wills, the wills of contemporary mankind, will remain for future generations, also in the guise of what we understand as nature. If the conception of nature as a representation takes hold of everyone, perhaps with this new will we will overcome the old, and nature will no longer exist. Dobrolyubov somehow derives from this theory his earlier conservative-gentry convictions. But what is better, he has written several splendid poems on the basis of these thoughts. [. . . .]

He left, and it was somehow lonely and sad. And suddenly I remembered: I had completely forgotten my sister Nadya. That is, I saw her look, pleading to go with us. But somehow I didn't grasp it—I just looked and didn't see—and just now remembered. Perhaps she cried. And I felt very sad.

August 13. Have finished my book on art: there it lies before me. Blessed be the life-giving pride of the creator! Great is the mystery of words and their power. Some are almost like silver trumpets in the field, others are created by visiting angels, still others are immobility itself and death. Happy is he who knows the incantations! At his sign, the desultory, harmonious hosts gather. Oh, the triumph of conquerors, marching with unfurled banners! The shouts of warriors are heard, the singing of trumpets . . . Blessed be the leader's pride, rising again to life. [. . . .]

August 20. Caught cold and am ill. I yield myself to the enveloping delirium—one of my favorite luxuries. O, deserted streets! A world of harmonious steps. I follow the outline of passionless shadows and listen, listen to a song-like murmur of talk. Softly lighted distances; the languor of a melody without harsh sounds. Ever deeper and deeper over firm stone slabs, as if into familiar waves, to the very bottom. To rest on serpents of tangled stalks, where there is glass, and ripples, and the nearness of space. I need no other country or reveries or mystery! Distant and superfluous are the phantoms of my recent sufferings. O deserted images, world of harmonious words! I yield to the enveloping delirium—one of my favorite luxuries. [. . . .]

August 29. We are in the city. It has all returned: the delightful wandering through narrow streets, along the walls of motionless houses, midst the night of public gardens coming alive . . . I roam and compose verses and remember Balmont, who has just published his *Stillness*.[26] It is all something that has been, something familiar, but which can come back to life if only for an instant.

Early September. Life in the world of thought: history and philosophy . . . A calibrated life.

September 12. Dobrolyubov suddenly turned up again. The three of us (Eda, Nadya, and I) were reading about Descartes; there was a ring, and he came in, completely different from what he had been before. I tried to start up a conversation with him, but he answered in monosyllables. Often we sat in silence. Suddenly with the words "I will pray for you," he rose and fell face down. We were unnerved. Eda turned white. I asked him: "To whom are you praying?" He answered: "To all pure spirits, earthly and heavenly" and to you "angels"—and he bowed to the ground four times, to

26. K. D. Balmont, *Stillness* [*Tišina*] (St. Petersburg, 1898).

the three of us and to our marriage. Eda was trembling and at one point almost fainted. During the final moments of the evening we were completely beside ourselves. With the words, "If I do not kiss your feet, you will not be with me in paradise," he kissed our feet . . .

He spent the night here. He passed the morning with us, then left, and returned, staying till about six o'clock. With long pauses he uttered the following words: "I pray for you morning and evening, you are always with me."—"O, do not force me to live too long in exile!"— "Everything is already finished in the heavens, now let the people only understand." "You said that you fear only one thing, my death, but how horrified you will be, learning of the death of my spirit."

Making our farewells, I said to him: "In truth you are hard for us to bear. As Simon Peter once said, I say to you: 'Depart from me, for I am a sinful man.' "[27] He apparently was struck by this and begged us: "Please let me be alone." When we came back, he spoke to us only about the death of his spirit. We said nothing, as if we were seeing him off to the grave.

He left us a bundle of papers.

Idem. Was at *Russian Archive,* turned in my Tyutchev article.[28] Saw Bartenev, the venerable elder, in an armchair with his crutches nearby. We had a nice talk

27. Luke 5 : 8.
28. Bryusov's first article for *Russian Archive,* "About a Collected Edition of the Works of Tyutchev," was published in 1898, no. 10, not no. 11, as the notes to the Russian edition of the *Diary* states. This error was carried over to the 1976 bibliography of Bryusov (see Selected Bibliography). Bryusov gives the title incorrectly. In his New Year comment below he refers to this piece and to translations of Tyutchev's letters in French to his wife, appearing in *Russian Archive,* 1898, no. 12.

about the Russian language, and he kept recalling Aksakov and Kireevsky. He is of course outraged at contemporary writers and their style: "Foreign words because the writer borrows his *thought* from foreign writers; anyone who clearly understands his *own* thought will express it in Russian." Then his son came, whom I like less.

September 16. Was again with Bartenev. We talked spiritedly about the three perduring Greats, Pushkin, Tyutchev, Baratynsky. But Pushkin is the greatest of these. [. . . .]

October 4. Have seen Balmont twice. Once was at Kursinsky's. Kursinsky had met Balmont the day before somewhere outside of town and invited him to lunch. The three of us recited poems, many poems, Shelley's, Dobrolyubov's, our own. But Kursinsky was a pest. When I recited "For the New Bell," he shouted in outrage, "But if that will do, we'll wind up putting the songs of beggars into our verses!"[29] O, *sancta simplicitas!*

I saw Balmont again yesterday. At the beginning there were four of us—we were with our wives. But afterward I went out to "see him home" (for about two hours)—and the past returned. Strange. The voice of Balmont, more readily than anything else, returns the past to me—the "me" of the times of *Me eum esse* and earlier, the times of "And once again" or "Snows."[30]

---

29. "For the New Bell," first published in *A Book of Meditations* (see note 33), appears in later editions as "Song of the Almsgatherers" ["Sborščikov"]. Its novelty lay in irregular rhythm, imitating the actual chants of these people.

30. Poems appearing in *Chefs d'oeuvre* ("And once again . . ." in the second edition only). During the period Bryusov refers to he was much under the influence of Balmont's personality.

There is always charm in the past, and, perhaps for that reason, I love to be with Balmont. *And once again* we roamed the nighttime streets under the black sky, in the fierce cold of early winter, and again we sat in the lighted hall of a restaurant, and it was as it had been "in the old days," only the Saturday organ was still. We told each other our best thoughts of these last years, and sometimes these mad creations of the imagination taken to its extreme limits became frightening. The "duality of the human body," ghostliness of the distances to the stars, "shades come from the moon"—oh, how feeble all of this becomes in words, and how full of meaning it was last night!

October 6. My little article ("Variants of Tyutchev") has appeared in *Russian Archive* (No. 10). Three years ago this would have given me great joy. In those days, I talked about my pride, but was not at all proud and very much desired the praise of my contemporaries. Now I do not repeat my bold words from the "Preface" [to *Me eum esse*], now I constantly apologize in my article . . . But that is only because I carry in my soul the awareness of my importance. And such small change as this little article doesn't even make my heart beat faster.

October 8. Balmont has gone. Sad without him. Sadder than I expected. Still and all, it's bitter to have no one who can listen to your poetry and to whose words and opinions you can pay attention. It's hard to be at the same time both creator and judge, and so year after year . . . [. . . .]

December 3. [. . . .] Received a letter from Dobrolyubov from the Solovetsky Monastery. "In the daytime a certain terror rules the weak body," he writes.

December 5. A letter from Balmont about my book. Ecstatic. "My brother, powerful one! I greet your remarkable book . . . It is full of thought as the mountain air is full of storms . . . Oh, I have always dreamed of you thus . . ." Except for this letter, my friends speak rather tepidly of my book [*About Art*].

December 8. Petersburg. I've seen Balmont twice, even three times. We examined the drawings of Goya and read Calderón. Kursinsky, who came with us, is visiting editorial offices and publishing houses. We also went to the Hermitage. Tomorrow at Balmont's there will be a gathering of poets, invited with me as the "main attraction."

December 9. Last night we were at a concert where Balmont recited verses. The combination of Balmont's poems and the public is of course painful. Afterward the three of us—Balmont, Kursinsky and I—went to Palkin's to drink some wine.

. . . Then we went to see Merezhkovsky, who is ill. In the beginning Zinaida Gippius gave us tea in a dark and dirty dining room. She didn't try to be pleasant and little by little began to insult me. I repaid her in kind, and I know that two or three blows went home. For example, she attacked Dobrolyubov. With the most innocent air I said, "But you know, it seems to me that in your poetry you imitate him."

Afterward we were allowed to see Merezhkovsky for a quarter of an hour. He lay undressed in bed. Right away he began to talk about my book and attack it fiercely.

"There's not even anything to attack because there's nothing in it. I agree with practically everything in it, but without pleasure. When I read Nietzsche, I tremble down to my toes; but this, I hardly know why I'm reading it."

Zinaida tried to stop him.

"No, let me be, Zinochka. I'm speaking straight from the heart, and you, even when you keep quiet, you sting like a serpent, which is even worse . . ."

And he really did speak from the heart; he abused, even more than me, Tolstoy, tossing around on the bed and shouting, "Leviathan! A leviathan of triteness!"

In the evening I was at Balmont's, where I found Minsky and Sologub. Minsky is a little spider-like man, with a black goatee and a bit of a Jewish accent. He spoke commonplaces and trivia . . . However, poetry also came up. Minsky agreed with my comments about meter, but so unnecessarily. I recited "For the New Bell" as an example; he praised it; I had to bow my head furiously, as if in gratitude, for there was nothing to argue about. Balmont asked if he had read my book. "I did." "And what was your impression?" "I expected something more revolutionary . . ." Finally he left.

Sologub as usual was silent most of the time, but later, after Minsky left, he livened up a little. Still later, when we were returning home together, we chatted. He spoke of Dobrolyubov: "Oh, I know him for what he is. He's still the same serpent, spellbinding but deeply false!" [. . . .]

December 11. All the poets attended Polonsky's funeral. Sluchevsky said to them: "The one at whose home we used to gather on Fridays is dead, now let us gather at my home." The poets call these Friday gatherings at Sluchevsky's their academy. I went there tonight with Balmont and Bunin. Following the custom,

I brought the host volumes of my poetry, sat down and began to listen . . . There were quite a few people there [. . . .] We three Decadents, Balmont, Sologub and I, hid ourselves dejectedly in a corner. [. . . .]

When everyone had gathered, they began reciting poems. Mazurkevich recited the greeting he wrote for the evening in memory of A. K. Tolstoy—"To Aleksey Tolstoy praise . . . Praise to Aleksey Tolstoy . . ." Balmont recited "Maya," and they completely failed to understand it. Gaideburov muttered something about richness of imagery . . . Balmont also recited his poem to Sluchevsky, who was flattered but "declined the honor." I recited "For the New Bell," and since it is assumed that I am a Decadent, everyone found this poem arch-Decadent. I had hardly finished when Safonov leaped wildly from his seat and shouted: "Gentlemen! this is the question: is this a searching for new ways or something else?"

Here everyone began to speak. I was going to put in two words, but to outshout Safonov isn't so easy. "I," he said, "worship poetry! I will not yield an inch!" I gave up and fell silent. Just then there crawled up to me a two-legged creature which began to speak: "I've read and heard so much about you, I'm very glad to meet you. I have an album graced with the autographs of many notable persons, won't you consent to grace it with this poem?"

I consented and graced it, but hardly had finished when the owner of the album, who turned out to be a German poet Fiedler, asked me: "And have you your portrait with you?" Of course I did not.

"Be so good as to send me one autographed. I have a portrait gallery of notable persons." Finally he handed me a calling card on which he inscribed: "Friedrich

Fiedler. (1) Portrait, (2) Books of poetry (all autographed)"![31] [. . . .]

After supper Safonov sang something, but by this time I was trying to get Balmont to leave . . .

And they say that this was their best evening, for Merezhkovsky wasn't there. Otherwise, he terrorizes the whole company.

O Words! The word cannot lie, for it is holy. There are no low words!

The old fellows are silent, fearing that Merezhkovsky will put them down with authorities and quotations, for these old boys aren't very learned. The young ones don't dare protest, but are bored; only Zinochka Gippius rides high.

From Sluchevsky's, five of us left together—Balmont, Safonov, Korinfsky, Mazurkevich, and I. But Mazurkevich, with his stupidly self-satisfied physiognomy and his beaver coat, was so unbearable that we hurried to get rid of him. Then the four of us went on to some tavern (Nemchinsky's, I think), where we drank beer.

Safonov sat opposite me and asked, in an attempt at a probing voice:

"Tell me, Bryusov, are you a charlatan or are you sincere?" I said something about the oddness of the question. "Oh, no, you don't! If I'd known that you'd wiggle out of it, I wouldn't have asked. Can't you answer straight?"

I had to smile and answer straight. [. . . .]

December 12. Saturday. This evening I took a book of poetry to Safonov. [. . . .] From Safonov I dropped by Sologub's. There were various people

---

31. In fact much later Bryusov did send Fiedler a snapshot of his portrait by Vrubel.

there—Vladimir Gippius, Minsky, Korinfsky, Lebedev (a wild and gloomy fellow), and a youngish student, Oreus. Balmont and I kept to the side. The most remarkable was the recitation by Oreus, for he is a splendid poet. Gippius also recited some fine poems. Minsky laughed jerkily and told some not very profound jokes. Sologub kept silence as usual and recited nothing, though he has some remarkable poems, especially his "Dawn Lovely Dawn." [. . . .]

December 14. This morning I went to see Oreus. A sickly lad, with nervous twitches. He recalls a little the Dobrolyubov of former days, but is less attractive. He is completely absorbed by the newest French poets, Vielé-Griffin, Régnier, Verhaeren . . . We didn't strike it off especially well. I got Dobrolyubov's manuscripts from him. [. . . .]

December 18. Moscow. Found many letters at home. Among them from *The Banner*. Nikolai Obleukhov regrets that he can't publish "Assarhaddon." I got angry and demanded all my manuscripts back. They were returned with a letter with all sorts of greetings. [. . . .]

Christmas. Was at Bachmann's. There were many ladies there, and in the end I lost my temper and stubbornly defended absurd things, such as Balmont being higher than Shakespeare, truth in art being unnecessary, etc. [. . . .]

On January 5, I had a soirée here for poets: Bachmann, Bunin, Durnov, Kursinsky, Savodnik, Lang . . . There were some obvious mishaps, like the wine, which turned out to be sour; but in general the guests seemed to be satisfied. —"We are so isolated," sighed Bachmann, "that to have the opportunity to talk about poetry is in itself happiness."

[New Year (?)]. But it is already the new year. Time to say good-bye to the old. For me it was a very good one, and I can only bid it farewell with gratitude.

A very bright year in my life! The Crimea, the article on art, the meeting with Dobrolyubov, articles on Tyutchev, the trip to Petersburg, many good poems— all that I can look back on. What the new one will be, with the gloomy name of ninety-nine, I don't know. But on New Year's Eve, when we were on the other side of the house, clinking glasses and celebrating in the family circle with a "Happy New Year," some "unknown culprits" broke into our entrance hall and stole five overcoats, including some brand new ones, which my wife and I just had made . . . That can hardly be called an auspicious beginning.

1899

January. I've given myself up entirely to peaceful occupations. I'm preparing with suitable deliberateness for the "official examinations," am tutoring my sisters, and in the evenings the three of us—Nadya, Eda and I—read Shakespeare. Sometimes I drop in to Lang's for some "spirit writing,"[32] and we also pop into the theatre (*Antigone*)—and that's all.

Balmont came to Moscow. We saw each other many times but were never close for a moment. At first, hopes were held out for the future, when Balmont would return

---

32. Bryusov's interest in spiritualism lasted a number of years.

from Shuya. But when he came back from Shuya, he left the same day for Petersburg . . . [. . . .]

Balmont gave a lecture on Calderón. In the hall of the Historical Museum, which seats six hundred, there were between fifty and sixty, all our own group. [. . . .]

Balmont and I spent the day of his departure together . . .

The most interesting things were the three notebooks of Oreus, which Balmont brought with him. We were all enthralled, reading, rereading, copying, learning by heart. I wrote to Oreus an ecstatic letter, though I knew in advance I'd receive a very reserved response. Balmont got the idea of publishing a book of poetry by Oreus, me, and others.[33] At first there were many participants, but Gippius and Sologub later backed out. They were apparently irked to find themselves in proximity to me and Oreus. Now there are four participants: Balmont, Oreus, Durnov, and I.

I don't know whether this collection will come out. I remember an anecdote about Mallarmé. At a picture exhibition a certain journal publisher met him and, being struck by his judgments, asked him to write art surveys for him. But when Mallarmé sent him such a survey, the publisher returned the manuscript with an indignant letter, saying he didn't know how he had deserved to be made fun of. The same thing with me. Obleukhov begged (and I do mean begged) me for some poems, but when he had them, he didn't publish them. Later Bunin wanted some for *Southern Review* and appar-

---

33. *A Book of Meditations* [*Kniga razdumij*] (St. Petersburg, 1899) contained poetry by Konstantin Balmont, Valery Bryusov, Ivan Oreus [pseud. Konevskoy], and Modest Durnov.

ently also hasn't published them. Will Balmont now publish them? [. . . .]

March. [. . . .] The poems I sent to Bunin were printed (barbarously) in *Southern Review,* no. 727. Of course, a newspaper is used for various household needs, and if I decide to publish there, it is only in order to be published somewhere. [. . . .] I was at Bartenev's again. O living archive! Dead men for us—Aksakov, Khomyakov, Vyazemsky, Tyutchev—for him these are all acquaintances, friends, or at the very least, contemporaries. If one were to write down everything he says, what a wealth of information that would be.

March 17–22. Trip to Petersburg. This is the first time Eda and I have been separated for several days; I felt it very keenly. In the train I fell in with an "intellectual" crowd that I couldn't bear. [. . . .] Balmont greeted me enthusiastically. I have long been amazed at his love for me, but one must believe in oneself! I've settled in some strange hotel on Pushkin Street, No. 2, but have spent most of my time with Balmont. He arranged an evening gathering for me with all sorts of notables. I've been fed lunches and dinners and fussed over in all sorts of ways . . . [. . . .]

Visited Oreus twice. He is just the same and keeps on writing the same kind of poems, over and over. Good but boring. You are talking with him and suddenly he interrupts: "I'm going to recite a profound poem for you." He doesn't even add that it's his own. That's to be understood. And he recites, recites, recites. [. . . .]

Not everyone whom Balmont had invited turned up. For example, Boborykin didn't come. Many left early. [. . . .] Merezhkovsky and Zina Gippius were the same as always. For instance, Gippius asked Balmont to recite his poem to Sluchevsky. He recited it. "Strange," she said, "the second time I like it less. That's the way with all your things, Konstantin Dmitrievich." And Merezhkovsky howled, "How banal!" Gippius recited a poem of Minsky's, "Cast Off the Old Chains," but Merezhkovsky refused to recite, saying that he knew nothing from memory.

I recited Pavlova's "Fire," Dobrolyubov's "Whether in the Morning," and Maeterlinck's (my translation) "Et s'il revenait un jour." The first they heard with attention and said: "Romanticism," "Beautiful," "Uneven," "Rhetoric." Zina got excited about my translation. "See, see [to her husband], here one stanza is missing and another is added." "Yes, yes," Balmont assured her, "It's bad, very bad." Dobrolyubov's poem caused a furor. Merezhkovsky set up a howl, "Oh, how banal it is!" Balmont rushed into argument with him, demanding what he meant by "banal." "Uninteresting commonplaces," clarified Zina Gippius. But the most excited was the venerable translator Weinberg. "I don't understand! I don't understand—'Am I a youth or a star,' what does that mean? 'Did I die long ago or do I live.'[34] What's that? I don't understand."

I got furious and pounced on him. "There's nothing here to understand! You may say it's banal, but not that it's incomprehensible. It is the most elementary philosophical thought, that there is no border between reality and revery, between life and death. The simplest idea in the world!"

34. From a poem of Alexander Dobrolyubov dedicated to Yakov Erlich.

I was so fierce that Weinberg babbled, "Well, that I can't understand, means that I'm stupid."

Sluchevsky said, "I would make a superb poem out of that." And he's right, he would. For he is very able. He recited his new poems, and they were remarkable, but he recites very badly, in a wooden voice, as if he were reading a report. But later they begged him to recite "When I Was a Priest of Memphis"—from his early poems—and he stood up straight and recited in a voice like a hammer, splendidly. He *knows how* to recite.

Balmont has a collection of Sluchevsky's poems, among them some really amazing, audacious things—for example, "Eloa." The other evening at Sluchevsky's, after downing three or so, Balmont seated himself beside him and started praising him. "You have some magnificent pieces, you yourself don't realize what you have created. We were reading 'Eloa,' and Bryusov said, 'Yes, yes! That's no Lermontov!' " Sluchevsky blushed, became confused, lost his composure and didn't know what to say. I had to intervene and explain that, really, his work was remarkable. "Well, today's demon is simply cleverer," said Sluchevsky, and he's right.

On that Friday, Balmont was to have read his translation of Marlowe's *Faust,* which he had completed in nine days (so that his hand had become inflamed from effort and was on the verge of paralysis). But hardly had we arrived when there appeared some man, thin, with a bloated face "framed" (yes, exactly) with reddish hair. It was Fofanov. He had brought with him a lengthy narrative poem.[35]

---

35. Konstantin Fofanov's narrative poem "An Unusual Romance," written in 1899, was published in Petersburg in 1910.

"Here," he said, waving his hands, "here are 101 stanzas in ottava rima, i.e., 808 lines. Ottava rima is a forgotten form. I have resurrected it. If nothing were resurrected, where would we be? I have resurrected it."

They seated him on a sofa, so that a cast-iron Pushkin stood with its back to him. "What's this, what's this," Fofanov began, "Pushkin turning his arse to me!" And there were ladies there (Lokhvitskaya, Chyumina, Allegro). So they turned Pushkin's backside to the ladies, and Fofanov began to recite. My God! what a poem, 101 stanzas of ottava rima about a poor military school student who disguised himself as a girl . . . 808 of the most naive lines! Everybody was a wreck. The evening was a wreck. My God! Was that really the same Fofanov? The person was right who called him a "galvanized corpse." He died, and a long time ago, too.

After the recitation Fofanov left quickly . . . People began to talk and stretch their legs after an hour and a half of sitting. Lokhvitskaya kept apologizing that she hadn't found a copy of her book for me. Merezhkovsky also came up to me to say a few words, obviously to smooth over his earlier outburst. Among other things he said, as if it were a revelation, "The hardest thing of all is to live as everyone else lives." I'd have had every right to howl, "What banality!"

Later they asked me to recite "Demons of Dust" [see the appendix]. I did so, to tell the truth, without enthusiasm. To my surprise, the poem was a great success. Everyone exclaimed that it was fine, interesting; and Merezhkovsky said, "There are original images," and began to debate with me why I consider demons of dust to be crimson. I argued for a long time and finally said stubbornly, "I refuse to believe in their grayness." Merezhkovsky said, "That was well said," and calmed down. I was asked to repeat it. I did so. Sluchevsky took the poem from me for the *Pushkin Anthology*. That was unwise on his part, for it contains a good deal that is too bold. However, two other editors are involved besides Sluchevsky.

After me Lokhvitskaya recited ("The Bumble-Bee," not a very good poem). Balmont refused to recite. "Why won't he recite?" Lokhvitskaya asked. "Probably from modesty," I said. "And why did I recite?" "Obviously you are less modest than he." [. . . .]

After the soirée, we three—I, Balmont, and Korinfsky—wandered around until 6:00 A.M. Like all "repetitions," this was unsuccessful. It was embarrassing that in every dive I would leave behind the copy of Korinfsky's "Hymn to Beauty," which he had presented to me, and he had to remind me every time. Balmont almost lost his *Faust,* like Leo Levborg in *Hedda Gabler.* [. . . .]

End of March. Moscow. [. . . .] In *Problems of Philosophy* there is a notice of my book, the kind you can live with. Sluchevsky sent me a letter saying that my "Demons of Dust" "wouldn't do," because the "verse texture" was impossible. I answered him with a disquisition on what the line means in verse.[36]

March 29. I headed for the university today. Students were milling around. There was talk of beating

36. Bryusov wrote to Sluchevsky on March 26, 1899: "I wanted to bring my verse as close as possible to that which the folk discovered, pondering for centuries over how best to compose a song."

up those who planned to take their examinations.[37]
[. . . .]

April. Went by the university again. The students are wandering around downcast because the ringleaders have been arrested. Police—masses of them everywhere, and Cossacks riding about, smirking, waiting for someone to give them permission to start using their whips. With the people and the troops in such a mood (for they despise the students), what sense is there in these "intelligentsia" disturbances! [. . . .]

April–May. Examinations. I'll say this, the examinations, "this ordeal," has put me to a great deal of work. Usually I've studied from ten in the morning or earlier till midnight or one. Including during tea and during dinner. I've reviewed every course twice and gone over everything in my mind. But since all of it was either stale and familiar or repellent because of its intellectual slant, these exams have been a torture. [. . . .] I studied for two solid weeks. Alarming rumors have been going around. The students have revolted and are threatening to beat up those who take the exams. Our emissaries have been to see the professors, who scared them with the severity of their requirements, especially Guerrier. I've exchanged letters with Savodnik about these calamities, and we both feel very low. Twice all of the examinees gathered (at my place) for discussion; ten or twelve came, strangers to one another or almost, and we drew up programs of study . . .

37. A student strike, which began in Petersburg in mid-March, provoked by the flogging of some students by police, spread to most Russian universities within ten days. The strike lasted over six months, and 949 students were expelled from Moscow University alone.

First came the written exams (26 and 28 April). Our emissaries went to find out the topics. Guerrier threw a fit: "Aren't these exams to be impromptu? Aren't they now?" But he allowed a list to be sent to him, telling what each was studying specially, so that we were all more or less prepared. I wrote something very nice on the theme "Rousseau," with a description of the eighteenth century, a survey of the condition of France before the revolution and Rousseau's influence on the revolution . . . I had two epigraphs: "Je n'avais rien conçu, j'avais tout senti" (J. J. Rousseau); and "Lascia le donne e studia la matimatica" (said to him).

Klyuchevsky, on the other hand, met our representatives very kindly and hinted that the topics would be either "The influence of the steppe on . . ." or "The Time of Troubles." But when we came to the examination, he gave just one theme (Guerrier had given seven): "The influence of Peter the Great's reforms on the economic life and the political structure of Russia." We were stunned. No one was prepared. We went to ask for another topic. After long pleading, Klyuchevsky took pity and assigned the topic: "Phenomena of Russian history of the thirteenth and fourteenth centuries." I wrote on that, rather poorly and routinely.

Then came a week of preparation for modern and medieval history. That was the most difficult time. No one was sure he had passed the written exams, everyone feared Guerrier, who nonetheless seemed to us a tyrant. Furthermore, I had no lecture notes and had to study from Kareev's history. And besides that, I was pestered by guests. Vladimir Gippius dropped by and stayed for three hours, recited a lot of poems and wondered why the journals print the poems they do. Then Balmont dropped by. Nevertheless, my fear of Guerrier was so great that I knew modern history superbly. The medieval period I knew less well but still not badly.

After a one-day rest came classics. This was hard. For me the worst exam was Greek. The only time I've ever received the grade "Satisfactory." The problem was that I hadn't translated the last chapter, counting on luck, and it was just that that Sobolevsky asked. On the other hand, I did brilliantly in Latin, even to giving variants. The general misfortune brought us examinees together. We really grieved over those who failed. We pitied one of the Shabliovskys, whom Vinogradov demolished because he didn't know Henry the Lion.[38] We especially pitied Trankvilitsky. This is a man over thirty, perhaps almost forty, who is employed somewhere (perhaps a postoffice clerk?) and studies part-time. He prepared well for everything but couldn't do classics. Sheffer, Sobolevsky and our chairman Nikitin tortured him for three-quarters of an hour each, regretted that he showed no sign of "knowledge of the language" and finally failed him. This was totally unjust because for us, the regular students, the exam in classics wasn't as rigorous, almost a joke: they asked us to translate at most only five or six lines!

The exam in Russian history was also difficult. [. . . .] All the rest was much easier. The exam in church history was rather ridiculous. [. . . .] The exam in philosophy was very pleasant for me, but I had to study, because it would have been shameful not to know something. [. . . .]

38. Henry the Lion (d. 1195), member of the Welf dynasty, was made Duke of Bavaria and Saxony by Frederick Barbarossa.

We who passed the exams planned a supper and an orgy, which ended rather disgracefully. Izvekov and I drank a toast to anarchism and afterward made a tour of the most disreputable dives. My head ached for the next two days. It took me a long time to recover from the exams. Went to see Lang in Kuskovo, then to Balmont at Banki (on the Ilinsky Highway), where we lounged about and then wandered around, and drank till five-thirty in the morning . . . We kept talking of the same things, of Cleopatra, of God, of lilies . . . Now we're getting ready to go to the Crimea.

June. Second trip to the Crimea. Like all repetitions our second trip to Alupka disappointed us in many ways. [. . . .] The only new pleasure this year was swimming. It is sweet—to yield oneself to the sea. [. . . .]

July. The end of our visit to the Crimea and it was crowned by the six-day hiking trip we made. [. . . .] I have few memories so joyful as of that trip. To live under the wide-open sky, to be "homeless" and not obliged to return, either today or tomorrow, to keep going forward—isn't that itself happiness! . . . To spend the night in the mountains on some miserable bench, along with two Tatars, wondering if they won't murder you during the night for your gold watch and revolver and throw you into a two-hundred-foot well in the caves . . . And the sweetness of desert footpaths with the fresh imprints where wild goats have slept, and to hear the cries of these goats, to hear the rustle of their flight. Even to get a glimpse of them running in leaps, frightened by the noise. [. . . .] Around all that, always, every instant—the splendor of Crimean scenes, gorges, precipices, ledges, mountain streams, stalactite caves, the endless stretch of vistas from the summit to Simferopol, to the Sea of Azov, and the broad, half-stony mountain pastures.

End of notebook. Let the twelfth notebook end with this, the notebook in which alone is concealed more happiness than in all the other eleven, with their dreams of childhood and youth. Yes, indeed, this cycle of my life has given me too much happiness and success! Speaking generally, I have succeeded in almost everything that I began, have accomplished a great deal of what I had expected these long, cold years. "And many a fair dream has been accomplished, / And I have no complaint against my fate . . ."

And another positive thing: all of this since Eda and I have been together. It will soon be two years since I last felt those mad, boundless attacks of depression which cut me off from life, which kept me from writing anything at all in this diary. Sanguine feelings, assurance, hopes—this is now my usual frame of mind. I have faith, I am at peace. I am making a quick review of all the successes of this notebook, or better, to begin earlier, from the day of our marriage. A week in Petersburg, our seven-day honeymoon, it's already far in the past, but bright, happy, joyous . . .

The stay in the Toulon and my first illness without Mama,[39] and the poetry that came back to me. [. . . .] The first trip to the Crimea, when I approached nature for the first time and for the first time understood what it means to love her, to breathe her, to yield to her. [. . . .] The days full of longing in Ostankino, where I

39. See note 20.

nonetheless wrote *About Art,* and where I once again met Dobrolyubov, also an event in my life. The accidental success with my Tyutchev article in the fall. After all the childish trifles, this was my first article to appear in a literary journal. Trips to Petersburg, acquaintance with the world of poets, which I had long desired. I should mention also my poems which Bunin printed in his paper. Whatever you might say, these were my first poems not printed at my own expense.

Success with examinations. It was a dangerous game I resolved to play. At the beginning, I was far from prepared and *might well* have failed. I risked a great deal, because *for me* to fail would have been very shameful. Everyone, everyone who knows me and who understood what was happening, as well as those who did not understand, would have regarded it as my fall. I don't know how I could have faced my acquaintances, those close to me and those remote, if I had "flunked." It was a great success.

Finally, the latest joy, the journey by foot among the Crimean mountains. Yes, like Polycrates, I am frightened by this surfeit of happiness. Where is the prayer that will preserve it longer and longer, so that my bliss the gods *comites conservent* . . . I fear for tomorrow. As for today, let my last word be a prayer: I thank you. [New notebook follows.]

July–August. Autumn has begun for me. We've returned to Moscow, to books, to studies, and only in memory there will unexpectedly flash gorges, foaming waves and wild goats. [. . . .] Balmont has come and immediately disrupted my routine. He turned up with some Polyakov and the Lithuanian poet Yurgis Baltrushaitis. Bachmann came too. Balmont recited verses and everyone went into ecstasies, because they were all really remarkable. [. . . .]

August–September. Several days went by slowly and quietly: I studied differentials, drew graphs, and went to the library of the Historical Museum to read old journals and literary miscellanies for my article on Baratynsky.[40] One day I came home to find Balmont and Sergei Polyakov. "Put on your dress coat and let's go—you're going to be a groom's man." I obeyed and we went to the station. Baltrushaitis and Mlle Olovyanishnikova were getting married . . . [. . . .]

Went to the city hall about military service.[41] Lately I've gotten so used to the idea of the barracks that I almost yearned for them. But they judged me "completely unfit." This might also qualify as a success, one of the successes of 1898–1899. *Gratias ago.* [. . . .]

October. Pertsov was here. He had some old news, of how six months ago on Easter Eve Diaghilev struck Burenin (i.e., slapped his face). Merezhkovsky is writing on Tolstoy and Dostoevsky.[42] I don't see why he bothers. Everything that he could say about them has already been said. [Bryusov's footnote: "I was mistaken. 1901."] [. . . .]

40. The article referred to is "About the Collected Edition of the Works of E. A. Baratynsky," *Russian Archive,* 1899, no. 11. It was the first of a series of articles Bryusov devoted to one of his favorite poets.

41. The conscription law of 1874 required every able-bodied male to enter military service at age twenty. However, several categories of service existed, with special privileges for holders of academic diplomas. University graduates might serve as little as three months.

42. Merezhkovsky's work *Tolstoy and Dostoevsky* was first published serially in *World of Art,* 1901–1902.

November. [. . . .] Working on old journals in the Historical Museum, I read Chernyshevsky's *What Is to Be Done?*[43] Whatever else one might say, it is an extraordinary novel, worth reading.

In general, a peaceful existence with my wife and my sister, a rhythm of occupations . . . "I rule my days, with order my mind is in harmony . . ." For now, I like it. [. . . .]

Still November. *Book of Meditations,* which we awaited so long and wishfully, has finally come out. It's out, but what will happen now I don't know. [. . . .]

November 19. In general, the last few months I have been intoxicated with Verhaeren. Polyakov was here (with Baltrushaitis) and preached Strindberg enthusiastically. Must read "Inferno," "Nach Damaskus," etc. [. . . .]

December 26. Not long ago we arranged a little jaunt outside the city, Baltrushaitis, Polyakov, Mme Sh., and I.[44] We went all around Sokolniki Park walking in the snow. I pressed Mme Sh.'s little fingers and she favorably responded. If I had even a little of my former urges, my former soul, akin to the great Spanish seducer, I could continue . . . But I'm bored. [. . . .]

---

43. Radical critic Nikolai Chernyshevsky's novel *What Is to Be Done?* [*Čto delat'?*] was published in 1864. Generally agreed to have little literary merit, it was nonetheless extremely popular and influential for several generations.

44. Despite his disclaimer, Bryusov's close relationship with Anna Shesterkina began at just this time and lasted about three years, with voluminous correspondence, a small part of which appears in *Literary Heritage,* 85 (see the Selected Bibliography).

New Year's. Polyakov long ago invited us to spend the holidays in the country. On New Year's Eve, Baltrushaitis stopped by and was particularly persuasive. I gave in. We hired horses and went . . . The evening of the first we had to spend at the factory of Polyakov's brother, where they put on a play, after which was a ball of the rural-merchant type, rather lavish. But two things made up for all that. First of all, the woods in winter, which I was seeing for almost the first time; the woods in winter and the skiing in them. [. . . .] Yes, somewhere in a wilder locality and in greater solitude, it would have been splendid. And the second thing: the drama *Tsar Maximilian,* which was presented by the factory workers.[45] Those parts which have remained intact from ancient times are splendid. The naiveté and triumphant stylization of it all produce an overwhelming impression. It "plucks the heartstrings" (as they used to say), in the scene when the shackled "rebellious son Adolf" sings: "I will go into the wilderness / Far from these splendid places . . ." By the way, that song was obviously inserted later. [. . . .]

1900

January. I passed the first few days of the year with Oreus and his friend Ivan Bilibin, a student who does illustrations of folk tales. We spent some time together, visited Lang, and met at my house. Then Oreus and I went to see some old churches—St. Vladimir-in-the-Old-Gardens and especially the Life-Begetting Trin-

45. *Tsar Maximilian,* a play for popular theatre dating from the early eighteenth century. Such plays were performed by soldiers and convicts, as well as factory workers. (Cf. the prisoners' performance in Dostoevsky's *House of the Dead.*)

ity, where the icon of the Georgian Mother of God hangs, and also four remarkable icons by Ushakov, the icon-painter for Tsar Aleksei. Standing an hour and a half in that cold, "summer" church, I caught a chill and am sick now.

January 12. Have just read *Resurrection*. Good, without any doubt. It is a summation of everything that Tolstoy has said at one time or another, his last will and testament. The beginning is better written. Toward the end he broke down under the weight of the material. There are some small contradictions (to say nothing of anachronisms, such as treating "Decadence" and the Tonkin expedition as simultaneous with *Notes of the Fatherland*).[46]

End of January, beginning of February. [. . . .] Bunin and Pertsov are in Moscow. Have seen Bunin three times or so. He is much deeper than he seems. Some of his thoughts on humanity, on the ancient Egyptians, on contemporary vulgarity and the shameful state of our science and learning—are even powerful and impressive. [. . . .]

Shrovetide. Somebody named Lev Amozov arranged an evening of new art (at the Sportsman's Club). He came and invited me to appear. But everything of my own that I wanted to read was forbidden by the special censor. So I recited something by Balmont. The hall was full, and most of my crowd was there (even without my invitation). When I came to the platform, they applauded. I recited "The Wilderness," with rather

---

46. Tolstoy's last novel appeared in 1899. The anachronism involved the contemporary movement, a historical event (1882–1885), and a journal which was published from 1839 to 1884.

lukewarm response, but "I Love You Bitterly, O Poor Deformed Ones" seemed to make an impression. As an encore I recited, "Oh, Yes! I am Chosen, Wise, Consecrated." However, to tell the truth, the program was a poor one. [. . . .]

April 19. Went to the Wanderers' exhibition (XXVIII); poor and boring.[47] Two things of Nesterov, a portrait by Repin, a few good features in drawings of Myasoedov, Levitan, Dosekin, and perhaps a picture by Shesterkin, nothing more. But Impressionism has invaded powerfully even here.

April 21. Thursday evening I got around a lot. First I was at Chernogubov's and talked about Fet. Then at Yury Bartenev's. There, besides Kozhevnikov, I saw Nikolai Fyodorov, the great teacher of life and rambunctious elder, from whose tongue both Vladimir Solovyov and Tolstoy have suffered. From the very start of the conversation I was taken with him. "One way or another, we all have to die," I said. "And did you take the trouble to reflect whether this is so?" he asked.

We talked about Nietzsche, and generally Fyodorov was hard on me. I enjoyed it very much, and when leaving (I was in a hurry), I thanked him. However, Yury Bartenev imagined that I was offended and sent me an apologetic letter. I finished the evening at Baltru-

47. A group of young artists broke away from the Academy in 1863 and, after some preliminary organization, formed the League of Travelling Exhibitions. They were called the Wanderers (Peredvižniki), and their work dealt most often with popular scenes and subjects from Russian life and history. Their first exhibit was in 1871, occurring thereafter almost annually. Bryusov refers to their twenty-eighth.

shaitis's, where I deliberately provoked the girls with my paradoxes. [. . . .]

May 23. [. . . .] Petersburg-Revel. In Petersburg I hoped to see Oreus and G. M. Dobrolyubov [Georges, sailor-brother of Alexander], but neither the one nor the other was there. Oreus had already gone with his father to Finland, and Dobrolyubov was on the S.S. *Poltava* at Kronstadt. At the Dobrolyubovs', I saw the youngest brother, little Konstantin, a naval cadet, it seems. While I was talking with him, a female figure peeked from behind the door. This was his mother, Maria Genrykhovna; she learned that I was Bryusov and got very exited. "Ach, forgive me. You knew my eldest son. I'm not dressed. You see, my daughters are graduating today from the institute and there is a ball. My eldest son respected you so. Ach, what a great misfortune! From the time he left here, neither I nor the children have gone to bed once without tears." She spoke with an accent.

She asked me to stay, and out of curiosity I went into the parlor. Having changed, she came in, chased out little Kostya, who was telling me something very nice, and again began talking about the "great misfortune."

"I do not speak Russian very well. My father was a Pole and my mother Danish . . ." We continued the conversation, mixing Russian with French. "You know, it's my own fault, I couldn't fathom him. But I am his mother! He was always so unusual. You know, he hadn't the least understanding of life. Whatever he wrote (I had no sympathy for it, but that's not the point), it was all on little slips of paper! If you dropped them, you couldn't put them back in order! He simply didn't know the value of money! He'd put it in one pocket and it would fly out the other; he'd give it away, spend it on sweets. Suddenly I'd get a bill from a bookbinder for eight rubles, or he'd order books from Deibner in Paris for eighteen rubles! I'd tell him 'I can't pay for it, I've got eight of you!' And that was enough so that he wouldn't speak to me for a week." (I imagine that these ruble figures were much exaggerated; Dobrolyubov must have spent very little.)

"And all the same, was this the career I wanted for him? What a blow it was! But again it was my fault. I didn't know how to handle the matter. He might have come part way. Yes? You noticed? When he spent that summer with us, I resorted to various subterfuges. Cooked him soup with meat. I don't consider that a sin. I deceived him and said that he was coughing and should drink honey . . . But he doesn't eat sugar. And can you imagine? He slept on bare boards. And why all that? Ach!" She lifted her big handkerchief to her eyes.

"You know, I made a big mistake. You, of course, heard that I put him in a mental hospital, the Preobrazhensky . . . He was completely isolated there . . . He saw none of the patients, only the doctor . . . But I admit, it was a mistake. My children rose up against me; my daughter announced then that she would enter a convent . . . He was there only ten days . . . If you write to him, be sure to tell him that I admit my mistake. We have a little estate in Poland . . . I can exchange it for some land somewhere near here. He can live there, and at least we'll know that he's alive. The way things are, it's eight months since I've heard from him . . . What a *Juif errant!*"

When we were parting, she asked, "Tell me, did he ask you for money?" I said no. Again she told how he demanded money from her once while on his journeys and took offence when she didn't send it. She pleaded with me to give her his address, but I managed to avoid it. As I left, she invited me to tea the next evening. She said that Georges might be there. Georges did in fact come for a few hours but found no one home, didn't know my address, and had to leave again. When I found out about that, I begged off the evening tea, saying that I had urgent business.

June–July. Revel is a northern Naples, *eine Weltstadt,* as Bartenev said.[48] The Revel Germans dote on their city. For them there can be no better. Unquestionably, Revel is a European city. It is self-sufficient, having in itself everything it needs. It could go on existing if the whole world fell apart. [. . . .]

We stayed in Revel two months. The first half of the time we lived alone, knowing no one, living quietly like Germans. In the mornings I translated the *Aeneid,* after dinner we read, sitting in the park, and in the evenings I worked on my autobiography;[49] and that is how it went, day after day. Finally, at the beginning of July, Peter Bartenev arrived, and with him his daughter, Tatyana. Our peaceful life was disrupted. We had to spend half of

---

48. Bryusov's pleasant, if slightly ironical, attitude toward Revel appears here and in letters to Anna Shesterkina and Yurgis Baltrushaitis. However, in the long poem "The Immured" ["Zamknutye"], first published entire in *Urbi et orbi,* he sees the enclosed, self-contained city as prototype of a future nightmare world totally controlled, glass-enclosed, and lifeless. He returns to this theme in his later story "The Republic of the Southern Cross," first published in *The Balance,* 1905, no. 12, and 1906, no. 1, and included in his 1907 volume *The Earth's Axis.* The image appears also in his unfinished play *The Earth* in the same volume.

49. *My Youth.* (See the Introduction and Selected Bibliography.)

each day with them (we dined together). And immediately Bartenev found work for us to do: copying the letters of Bulgakov for the printer.[50]

During that month I got to know Bartenev in private life for the first time. Sea baths, summer rest and walking braced him up, put him in high spirits. He not only recounted endless tales from his store of memories, not only recited whole pages of Pushkin, Tyutchev, Zhukovsky, Batyushkov, Derzhavin from memory, but he turned out to be unusually sociable. He could strike up a conversation with anyone he met and in such a way that that person would pour out to him his most intimate secrets.

The manuscript of *Tertia Vigilia* has been at the censor's and undergone cruel excisions. Yury Bartenev, who has just been made a Moscow censor, returned it to me with very odd comments. [. . . .]

July–August. Moscow. Right away, and more strongly than I expected, I was seized by the usual Moscow impressions, the whole circle of friends. Lang (who is now staying in our house) presented himself first. Then soon, very soon (by chance), came Polyakov, Baltrushaitis and Balmont himself.

Vladimir Solovyov is dead. Bartenev knew him well, and I went to the funeral with him. Thus, as fate would

---

50. The letters of Alexander Bulgakov, head of the Moscow post office in the early years of the nineteenth century, to his brother, who held the same position in Petersburg. The letters gave an excellent, informal picture of Moscow life of the period, beginning with 1812 and extending into the 1840s, all the more since Bulgakov had the habit of reading letters that came through his hands. The correspondence began appearing with 1900, no. 5, of *Russian Archive* and continued well into 1902.

have it, I met the critic of my first poems.[51] And I had dreamed—often, at that—of personal conversations. "But he would have charmed you," Bartenev said to me. I kissed the hand of my chance enemy, the poet and thinker whom I revered. Bartenev proposed that I write an article on the poetry of Vladimir Solovyov.[52] [. . . .]

End of August. I had a party at my house: Balmont, Bachmann and his wife, Polyakov, Baltrushaitis and his wife, Yury Bartenev, Lang, and Bunin, who dropped in by chance. Balmont recited poetry without end ("The Artist-Devil"). As Balmont put it so well, Yury Bartenev was the hyena, who, according to an African superstition, can sometimes speak in human language. We went on till 4:00 A.M.

Bunin has sold the manuscript of his poems to Scorpion, and I'm reading them. Am reading the proofs of *Tertia Vigilia.* Also reading mounds of proofs for *Russian Archive.* I am a journalist by calling, and I take delight in all this talk with the printers about layout, etc.

We saw Balmont off.

September. Am assiduously attending spiritualist Wednesday meetings. I preach, teach, and wield a certain influence. Once, when we were coming out of such a meeting, the neophytes began to thank me. "Since you've been coming, a great deal has changed. Before it was just Christian propaganda. For hours on end they kept telling us what the fluid is when it separates from the body. But now they are afraid of you . . ." [. . . .]

---

51. On Solovyov's criticism of Bryusov's first printed poems, see the Introduction.
52. "The Poetry of Vladimir Solovyov," *Russian Archive,* 1900, no. 8.

September 28. Bunin is in Moscow again. He tells how in Petersburg Merezhkovsky berated Scorpion: "I'm sick and tired, I can't bear it! They are mental onanists, gravediggers, I can't stand it any more!"

I dreamed last night of an end for *Brothers Karamazov*. [. . . .]

End of September. The miscellany planned by Scorpion has for some reason captivated Bunin, and he has started chasing after writers. We've become "Miscellanists." Bunin wrote to Maxim Gorky, who answered, "A miscellany? Can do."[53]

It was Saturday, I think, when we saw Gorky at the Grand Moscow Hotel. As always he was in a peasant shirt. A peasant-style moustache. Half-deliberate coarseness of speech. We dined together. "But I won't go into the main dining room, they'll gape. We drown in our own fame, like frogs in a swamp." Later he said, "Time to spoil my reputation. I'm tired of it!" And: "Only let's have no talk of social issues!"

He clasped my hand very hard and asked me to send him my book. "I've been hearing about you for a long time. I'm real interested. Bunin here recited some of your things to me. Good stuff." Bunin and Yury Bartenev are the most enthusiastic propagandists of my poems. [. . . .]

October. A short list of whom I've seen.

At the Shesterkins' I saw Mikhail Solovyov (the brother of Vladimir) and his wife Olga Mikhailovna, translator of Ruskin and Wilde. She is more interesting

---

53. Scorpion publishing house was founded in 1900 by Sergei Polyakov. *Northern Flowers* (1901) was the first of several miscellanies publishing modern writers. (See the Introduction for Scorpion's importance to the Symbolist movement.)

than he. I acted the "aphorist" very skillfully before them and managed to amaze them. She is dying to work for Scorpion.

After the performance of *Foam,* an interviewer, one Zhdanov, visited us Decadents.[54] I was going to receive him very pompously and began to put on airs, playing the role "Valery Bryusov," but it turned out that he amounted to more than I thought. I showed him Verhaeren: "Ah, I know," he said, "the Belgian poet." I showed him Agrippa [von Nettesheim], and he started to read it in Latin. He saw *Parnaso italiano* and began speaking to me in Italian. I was abashed. That was his book, it seems, under the initials "L. G." The interview appeared in *Russian Bulletin.* The best things were said, of course, by Durnov.

I saw Durnov a couple of days ago. He was in great form, put forth better aphorisms than I and better than Wilde, so that I inwardly applauded everything he said.

Have seen a good deal of Polyakov. Since Baltrushaitis left, he has been devoting his spare time to me, and in any case our activities turn out to coincide. Besides seeing him in the daytime, I was with him at some family celebration, then he came to me with Shesterkin, and finally, snatching him from the Wednesday spiritualist meeting, I carried him off to the Praga Restaurant. We drank and talked. Again for an instant he showed what he really is—other-worldly, deep . . . but only for an instant . . . My book has come out, but a strange indolence keeps me from getting to it; it bores me.[55] [. . . .]

I was at a literary soirée at Mme Varvara Morozova's.

54. *Foam* [*Nakip'*], melodrama by Peter Boborykin.
55. *Tertia Vigilia* (Moscow, 1900), Bryusov's third independent volume of poetry, usually said to mark the beginning of his maturity as a poet.

Savodnik gave a paper on Vladimir Solovyov. There were various liberals there: Ermilov, Peter Kogan, etc., and then some silent students, some of whom are my readers. There were also several actors from the Moscow Art Theatre.[56] Of course, they soon forgot Solovyov and, since I was present, began arguing about Symbolism. I was quite controlled and said nothing more pointed than, "This is an elementary truth, and if you wish I can explain it to you," or "If you don't understand, I can't help you." They seemed to be satisfied with me.

At the spiritualist seances, I experienced the sensation of trance and clairvoyance. I am a man who is rational to such a degree that these few instants which tear me away from life are very precious.

Maxim Gorky

We heard that Gorky was in Moscow, and because of the miscellany started chasing after him. Posse is protecting Gorky and won't let him out of his sight for a minute. Baltrushaitis saw a train somewhere: Gorky was in it, surrounded by Posse, Skirmunt, and someone else. We thought we'd see him Sunday at the Grand Moscow, but in vain—we passed our time over a bottle of wine. We drank the wine, the conversation became vital for a moment . . . but something broke it up and we all scattered. We learned for certain that we might see him on Monday at 10:00 A.M.

The night before, Yurgis [Baltrushaitis] was at the Art Theatre and saw him. And indeed everyone was gaping at Gorky. They wouldn't let him through the lobby.

---

56. Moscow Art Theatre, founded in 1898 by Konstantin Stanislavsky and Vladimir Nemirovich-Danchenko.

Students were screaming, begging him to say something. Finally, Gorky said: "I can understand that one might stare at the *Venus dei Medici* or at a drowned body . . . but why me? I came here to see *The Seagull*—something of unquestionable spiritual importance, and here you are, bothering about trifles."[57]

There he told Yurgis that on Sunday he would be at Vasnetsov's, but that he'd see us on Monday. We drew lots, and it fell to me to go look for him first. I got up very early for me and went. Along the way, I took five minutes to buy his book of short stories which I wanted to give to N. with his autograph. When I arrived, I asked the servants, "Is the gentleman in No. 70 in?" "No sir, just left." I cursed myself for being late. "I'll wait." "He probably won't be back for a while, sir." "No matter, I'll wait till evening." "Well, sir, he left no word. He may not even come back tonight." "I'll wait all night." The servants were confused and went away. I went into the room, sat down, feeling awful, and read *New Times*. Time passed, hours and hours. I was in despair. Suddenly I remembered that Gorky was not in No. 70 but No. 90. I ran headlong, burst into the room, and saw Gorky, Chirikov, Posse, Baltrushaitis and Mme Chirikova. I shouted something and started to explain incoherently to these people I hardly knew that I had sat an hour in No. 70. They smiled. I went after my things. The servants grumbled at me.

I insinuated myself into the general conversation, at first talking disconnectedly. Gorky was saying that he

57. In fact the play was Chekhov's *Uncle Vanya*. When the crowd tried to break into the box where he sat, Gorky sent them away in no uncertain terms and later was forced to justify his behavior to the newspapers.

envied people who know many languages. "And I," I said, "envy people who have experienced a great deal. Most of all, I envy you, Alexey Maximych."

He protested.

"Could you live twenty years among books and only books?" I asked.

"Of course not, that's impossible. I couldn't."

"I can't either, but in fact I have."

The conversation steered—of course, I steered it—toward various mysteries of morality. Gorky came to life and started to tell stories: Volga legends about Stenka Razin, who killed a monk whom he asked to pray for him, and some Belorussian folktales . . . I referred to my "Tale of a Bandit." Gorky recited it aloud. Posse and the others made faces.

Later, under cover of the general conversation, Gorky and I had a separate chat. "Not long ago I reread [my] *Foma Gordeev*," he said, "just casually, as if I'd stumbled on it. Ech, it's awful! So much that's superfluous, not simply told. I read a third of the way through and threw it aside . . . What's disgusting is these various human inventions, starting with the pavements and ending with the idea of God. Of course, I, a sinful man, walk the streets and sometimes pray to the Lord God, but that's all wrong."

He talked a lot more in the same vein, and Chirikov asked, "And consequently you don't think art is necessary?" Gorky began to prove to him that there is no "consequently" about it. Later, a conversation on the side between Baltrushaitis and Posse led to the reading aloud of a story of Baltrushaitis. In it he portrays the horizon's circle as something torturesome and destroying, as the boundary from which one cannot break out.

"Well, I've seen that circle," said Gorky, "and felt

differently about it. I wasn't frightened that I couldn't break out of it. Instead I always rejoiced that I, I myself, stood in the very center of that circle, and everything else was around me."

And we spoke about Shakespeare, about Pushkin, about Tolstoy, about Dostoevsky. "Here's what I prize in Dostoevsky," said Gorky. "You remember in *Notes from Underground,* the first part, that fellow who, when general well-being would come, would suddenly say: and why don't we send all this to the devil?" And with a movement of his foot, Gorky showed how that fellow would throw all that bliss into the abyss. He himself is capable of that.

Trip to Petersburg [. . . .] In Petersburg [Polyakov and] I went straight to the Balmonts'. We didn't find Balmont, but we looked around the room. A good many books: the Royal Shakespeare, thick volumes of Spaniards, Shelley, Poe. On the table were galley proofs of a history of art, books for an article on monsters and Paulsen on Kant. Then Balmont came and seemed glad to see us. He began to talk about the Scorpion crowd and some publications. We decided to go that day to the Minskys'. But we didn't have a copy of my book with us [*Tertia Vigilia*], so we went to a bookstore. In *New Times* [Suvorin's bookstore] they wanted to sell us *Chefs d'oeuvre,* which was on the counter; obviously someone had asked for something of mine. We found [my new one] at Wolf's.

Minsky wasn't home. Mme Minskaya greeted me rather sarcastically[58]:

---

58. Bryusov's rather light flirtation with Mme Minskaya (Lyudmila Vilkina) began with this meeting. Their correspondence throws interesting light on his character, but his attitude toward her was often ironical.

"So that's what you're like. Konstantin Dmitrievich told me you were blond."

"I never said that," protested Balmont.

"It's no doubt better that I'm not as you had imagined me," I said.

"Why better? Go ahead, then, and turn out more interesting than I'd imagined!"

Minsky arrived. I recited some of my poems. [. . . .] While saying good-bye I inscribed my book, and Mme Minskaya said to me: "Love what is frightening." Not understanding, I thought that she said, "Love frightfully," and I told her I was incapable of loving anyone. An unpleasant misunderstanding.

In the evening we saw the Siamese ballet.[59] Not savage enough. [. . . .] [Monday evening] we went to the Merezhkovskys'. They greeted us, as though we were buying their goods, as sweetly as you please. Andreevsky was there, and some other people, but they devoted themselves entirely to us. Dmitry Sergeevich showed me his library on Leonardo da Vinci and Peter I, and paid me various compliments: "You're an intelligent man, you're an educated man. I'm beginning to like your poetry . . ." Then he preached a lot about how now is the time of unification. All those seeking new paths must unite. But the highest value is religion. Anything new which is alien to religion does not deserve to live . . .

When we were alone, Polyakov asked Zinaida Nikolaevna for some stories. She drawled:

"And is this a miscellany for cha-a-aritable purposes?"

"No."

59. The Siamese ballet was a touring company playing in Petersburg. Rozanov wrote an ecstatic review, found in his book *Among Artists* (St. Petersburg, 1914).

"And will there be ho-no-ra-ria?"

"Yes, and good ones."

"Did you hear that, Dmitry, they're paying honoraria." Zinochka gave us two things: "Holy Blood" and "Those Who Came Too Early." [. . . .] —All this time I was on bad terms with Balmont. He doesn't like my new poems, nor I his. It went as far as nasty scenes and bitter words . . . [. . . .]

December. Moscow. In Moscow I was caught up in the usual life. Tuesday was drunken and full of poetry with Durnov . . . Thursday at Morozova's, where I gave a lecture on "the new art." Ivan Ivanovich Ivanov was there; he was elected chairman of the meeting, and he attacked me fiercely. For some reason I was too lazy to defend myself (was it worth arguing with him? and besides I was too tired from Petersburg). Too bad, because afterward he blabbed everywhere that he had worsted me on all points, and that my wife almost wept from despair . . . [. . . .]

The holidays. Everyone has gone away for the holidays. I attended the Wednesday seances, but there was nothing and no one of interest there. Kursinsky and Stanyukovich were in Moscow, but I saw them only fleetingly. More interesting was a gathering at Doctor N.'s, where Yurgis repeated his treatise on D'Annunzio. And before that a student named Chulkov read the beginning of his paper on my poetry. I didn't expect to live to hear such evaluations, and even less did I expect to be present personally at the reading of such a paper. Apotheosis in one's lifetime.

A new year, a new century. Since childhood I have dreamed of this twentieth century, trembled, seeing it in

Lentovsky's portrayal.[60] And here it is. —When you come right down to it, this winter is not a success: it's been divided between work with Bartenev for *Russian Archive* and rendezvous with Sh[esterkina]. Both annoy and repel me. Both will look better in a biography than they were in life. Time to break free!

1901. The New Century

January 15. Yesterday at Morozova's Chulkov read his paper about me, very ecstatic but very superficial. I was the first to pounce on the author and attacked his paper ferociously . . . Everyone, even my obvious ill-wishers, rushed to defend poor, disheartened Chulkov and, in defending him, they also defended my poetry. Yashchenko said some quite sensible things.

Gorky wrote that he isn't giving us a story for the miscellany. He claims that he can't write anything. Polyakov is indignant.

In Yasinsky's journal there was an article about me, very "sympathetic."[61]

Balmont has come to Moscow. At our first meeting we almost fell out completely . . .

February–March. Life (i.e., literary) has become concentrated almost totally around the miscellany. [. . . .] On miscellany business, I've corresponded with Pertsov, Rozanov, Oreus, D. Fridberg . . . All the

60. Mikhail Lentovsky (1843–1906), actor and director, was called the "magician and wonder worker of the theatre." Among other enterprises he founded the Moscow Fantastic Theatre, noted for boldly imaginative stage design.

61. *Monthly Essays* printed a review of *Tertia Vigilia* in 1900, no. 12, and an article "A New Poet" in 1901, no. 1. Reference is probably to the latter.

"prominent" writers gave us things that had been rejected elsewhere or forbidden by the censors. Zinochka Gippius gave us [a play] "Holy Blood," rejected by *Life* and *World of Art;* Rozanov gave us "Notes," which Pertsov had refused to print; Chekhov gave us a story which he had doubts about the censor passing,[62] and finally Minsky contributed a sonnet which the censor had cut out of his *New Songs*. This last, incidentally, we didn't print. There's been a lot of bother connected with the printing. The last few days we've read two or three proofs a day. Sergei [Polyakov] would drop by the printing shop about three times a day, and I every day without fail. Even the drunken Tuesdays at Scorpion have become sedate and are largely devoted to business. [. . . .]

April 6. My article was published in *Monthly Essays*.[63] Today I was invited by Sergei Diaghilev of *World of Art* to become a contributor. "So the wave wafts me / will-lessly upward."

April. [. . . .] At some public meeting Balmont recited a poem about the massacre in Turkey.[64] An official report was drawn up about it. His place has been

62. Chekhov's story "At Night" ["Noč'ju"], later published as "At Sea" ["V more"].
63. "Toward a Theory of Anecdotes," 1901, no. 4.
64. Balmont's "The Little Sultan," ostensibly prompted by a massacre in Turkey, was in fact occasioned by the beating of students by Cossacks at a demonstration near the Kazan Cathedral in Petersburg, March 4, 1901. Balmont was exiled from "the capitals and the university cities" for two years. Gorky signed a protest about treatment of the students and was arrested in Nizhny Novgorod in April for alleged acquisition of a mimeograph for publication of subversive material. Tolstoy was excommunicated from the Orthodox Church in February. His reply to the Holy Synod was dated April 4, 1901.

searched. Now they are talking of nothing but him in Petersburg. Gorky is in jail. Tolstoy is writing a protest to the Holy Synod. "All is seething with the spirit of opposition," to use the words of Fet.

    End of June. As it happens I haven't made any entries for a long time. The move to the dacha, isolated life in the country, constant trips here and there—and as a result, blank pages. Halfheartedly I looked up Balmont. A couple of times he sent me invitations from restaurants, once from the Hermitage, when the Scorpions were sitting with Merezhkovsky and Zinaida Gippius, but his notes didn't catch me. Then even the notes stopped. Balmont has devoted himself to the past. "And wild drunkenness, the plague-like vice of Russia, etc." Suddenly I got a telegram from Polyakov: "Mont (Balmont's nickname) is leaving tomorrow for a long time. Be at Sabashnikov's tomorrow at two." Naturally I flew there. Balmont is being exiled "from the capitals and the university cities and their provinces" for two years, all because of those lines about the "little sultan." For the time being he's going to the Sabashnikovs' in Kursk province and later abroad. Of course there had to be a send-off. First at Sabashnikov's, then at the Praga, still later at the Mauritania and Yar, the next day at the Slavyansky Bazaar and at the station. Incidentally, Balmont isn't drinking. Of course he's just the same. I recited my poetry. Referring to "Along Narrow Streets," he said, "That's the theme of a future book of mine." "Plagiarism again?" asked Polyakov. Balmont himself recited some weak poems. Of course we exchanged a farewell kiss. "For the first time now I see *you,* as you used to be," he said to me. [. . . .]

[N. N. Chernogubov] claims that Countess Tolstaya invited him to Yasnaya Polyana to sort out the archive.[65] Not waiting for the (probably casual) invitation to be repeated, he went. He was there five days and returned, though there had been talk of the whole summer . . . However, they let him have Fet's letters to Tolstoy. He has interesting things to tell about life at Yasnaya Polyana and about the immense hypocrisy there. The servants kowtow before "His Excellency," receive petitioners rudely and send them scraps from the master's table. "A person who's not an intellectual," the Count said once, "doesn't know how to explain what it is that he needs." Tolstoy talks a great deal against the Russian government. "If we could send it to the devil's granddam, everything would be fine." Chernogubov was about to get into an argument with Tolstoy, but that is against the rules at Yasnaya Polyana, where only Tolstoy makes pronouncements.

"What is it that you like in Fet?" asked the Count.

"Why, everything, the poet and the man."

"He was a bad man."

"But why? He was a genuine nihilist, and if he didn't believe in anything, he said so."

"The inability to constitute a faith for oneself shows a low soul."

"But it's not so simple. 'Life is a confusion and a complexity.' "

"Nothing confused about it. Before each person there is a handle. Grasp it, move it, and what will happen, the Master knows."

---

65. Chernogubov was working on a biography of Fet and turned to Countess Tolstaya, requesting her assistance. He was allowed to copy letters from Fet to her and to her husband.

According to Chernogubov, Tolstoy also spoke about me: "He began writing as a joke. They took him seriously, so he began in earnest." [. . . .]

Balmont told me that *World of Art* is dissatisfied with my article against Andreevsky.[66] "They need an article with sting in it." Zinaida Gippius said, "Bryusov wrote a ba-a-ad article, he started with Adam."

Since Balmont has left "the capitals," he can't write his literary survey for the [British] *Athenaeum,* so he delegated it to me.[67] All my life I've followed everything that is happening in Russian literature—except *this* year. But I got something together in five days, because the deadline was near. [. . . .]

September. [. . . .] About Oreus's death.[68] His uncle wrote, asking if I knew anything about him: he had disappeared. In turn I asked that they send me any news. Shortly his father wrote to me that he had drowned, swimming in the Aa. "If you are a believer, pray for his soul, pure as a child's." I began a correspondence with his father, with the idea of publishing his son's writings.[69] [. . . .]

Met Chulkov on the street. He praised to the skies Leonid Andreyev's story "The Wall," but I don't believe in Andreyev and I'm not going to read it. [. . . .]

66. Reply to S. A. Andreevsky's article "The Degeneration of Rhyme." Bryusov's "Answer" asserted that the innovations which Andreevsky attacked marked a new stage in the development of poetry. Both pieces appeared in *World of Art,* 1901, no. 5.

67. *Athenaeum,* no. 3847 (July 20, 1901).

68. Ivan Oreus drowned in the river Aa near Riga and was buried by local inhabitants as an unknown victim. His identity was established some time later. Bryusov visited his grave in the company of Nina Petrovskaya, who recounts the trip in her memoirs.

69. Ivan Konevskoy [Oreus], *Poems and Prose* [*Stixi i proza*], ed. Valery Bryusov, (Moscow: Scorpion, 1904).

Mikhail Solovyov came to see me, thanked me for my article on Vladimir Solovyov and brought me the first volumes of his collected works. Besides that, he offered something for [the miscellany] *Northern Flowers*.[70] Later I went to see him. His wife, Olga Mikhailovna, "worshipper and priestess of beauty," chattered charmingly about Fet and Vergil. There was also some general who was *peu lettré*, but who had been in the Khiva campaign and there read Tacitus while riding a camel. Solovyov's son the young Sergei also talked pleasantly about Corneille and Racine. —They were expecting the son of Professor Bugaev, a youth [Andrei Bely] who is a would-be Decadent and eager to see me. But it happened that he wasn't home (he lives nearby).

Bunin arrived in Moscow and came to see me. He said he was stuck in Yalta, suddenly became lonesome, and, not waiting for the ship he had been going to take, galloped off to the North.

At the Scorpions' Tuesday, I again talked hostilely to him. I said that none of his writing did anyone any good, the main thing was that it was boring, etc. He was magnanimous and praised my poetry all-round.

I received a letter from Lt. Gen. Oreus, Oreus's father, thanking me for my article in *World of Art* and agreeing to the edition.[71] [. . . .]

October. Running around to get the material for *Northern Flowers*. We've been three times to Chekhov without getting to see him. He lives in a little cottage

---

70. *Northern Flowers* for 1902 has no contribution by Solovyov.
71. "Wise Child" ["Mudroe ditja"], *World of Art*, 1901, no. 8–9. The article also appeared as foreword to the volume mentioned above, note 69.

practically in the sticks. The door was unbolted by a woman with her skirts tucked up. "No one here." "But perhaps he is home?" "Would I lie to you? He's gone out. If he were here, I'd have said so."

Also have been to see Andreyev. I didn't find him, only saw the apartment. Common, middle-class place, right down to the little pictures on the wall and a little couch. [. . . .]

November. Akim Volynsky-Flekser came to give a lecture on contemporary literature. The lecture was full of personal sallies but not devoid of some fine characterizations. When he reached the point of saying that Mikhailovsky was a liberal gendarme standing guard at his little railroad junction and allowing the trains of modernity to pass, the hooting began. It was done by two girl students, but their hoots were drowned out by applause. The same thing happened after the lecture. Some newspapers wrote it up differently, but their accounts weren't true. After the lecture, the students were terribly upset, and argued to the point of quarreling. Polyakov and I invited Volynsky to the Hermitage afterward and feted him. Later we went to Yar. We drank a good deal. Flekser was charmed both by Yar and by the troika (actually only two horses). He kept saying, "Petersburg has nothing like this . . ."

We bought an article on poetry from him for a hundred rubles.[72] He was delighted, clasped our hands and spoke warmly of Scorpion. He's very eager to run a newspaper.

Merezhkovsky's lecture was forbidden, both the

---

72. "Contemporary Russian Poetry" ["Sovremennaja russkaja poezija"], closing item in *Northern Flowers* for 1902.

Tolstoy and the Dostoevsky parts. I'm seeing what I can do, with the help of Yury Bartenev . . . After my efforts, Merezhkovsky is writing me sweet letters, calling me "dear" and signing himself "Yours." [. . . .]

December. The Merezhkovskys were in Moscow for five days. We Scorpions were with them all the time. In the daytime, from two to four, we lunched at the Slavyansky Bazaar, where they were staying, and in the evenings we went somewhere with them. Now and then, between meals, we paid joint calls with them. From the first encounters, they flabbergasted us with their Christianity. The first day, Thursday, December 6, was a holiday. Polyakov and Yurgis stayed home, and I had to take care of the guests alone. One had to keep them entertained all the time, without relaxing a moment. Remembering the mockery and abuse I had had from them before, I was cautious. But, to the contrary, the Merezhkovskys were more than friendly, falling over each other to praise my poems, reciting their own, arguing, asking advice. As previously agreed by letter, I arrived at twelve o'clock. I walked in, and the first thing I see is Zinaida Nikolaevna undressed. Of course I had knocked, received a "Come in," but the mirror was so arranged in the corner that it reflected the whole bedroom.

"Oh! We aren't dressed, but sit down."

We chatted between the rooms, then Zinochka (that seems to be what everyone calls her) entered. "I'm not going to do my hair, do you mind?"

Actually, she may not have done her hair, but she had nonetheless gathered it quite cleverly *à la chinoise.* We began talking.

"I don't know your Moscow customs. May one go anywhere in white dresses? Otherwise I don't know what I'll do. My skin somehow won't take any other color . . . In Petersburg everyone knows me this way. Because of this we don't go to the theatre. Everyone points at me . . ."[73]

Merezhkovsky came out, thanked me for my bother on his account and began directly with the necessity of believing in Christ. "One thing or the other: either you confess him to be God, then you are a true superman, or, if not, then you are not a mystic." He recited his poems, all about Christ and the Last Judgment, rather poor. Then Zinochka recited some splendid ones. "And the heart like a needle . . ."

In the evening, we went to the Solovyovs (as it happened, I had been there the night before). Zinochka again wore white, with a diadem on her head, arranged so that a diamond fell on her forehead. She knew Olga Solovyova only through correspondence. Meeting for the first time face to face, they didn't awfully care for each other. Olga Mikhailovna didn't find Zinochka as beautiful as she expected, and Zinochka found her too "esthetic." They talked about beauty. Dmitry Sergeevich inveighed against beauty, against Decadents, etc.

The preaching against Decadents struck everyone particularly, coming from Zinochka. She herself told, how at a lecture of D. S.'s at Petersburg University, one student said to her, "How painful to hear this from *your* lips." But they are against Decadence, they are for religiousness. Dmitry Sergeevich says that there is a schism in *World of Art,* because the literary section is now clearly

73. Gippius was a striking redhead.

religious, while the artistic section is still purely esthetic.

They talked a great deal about Rozanov. Mikhail Solovyov can't stand him, considering him an enemy of Christianity. "So apparently he got around you, too," he said to me, learning that I like Rozanov.

Zinochka shamed me. "It seems to me that you have become resigned. There is in you the very worst thing, self-satisfaction. For you everything is settled and cleared up." Look at the pot calling the kettle black!

Two of our student-Decadents: Boris Nikolaevich Bugaev (author of the *Symphonies* and son of Professor Bugaev), and Petrovsky, slightly stuttering. Bugaev tried to say very Decadent things. They both were in awe of Merezhkovsky and Zinochka.

The Merezhkovskys left at eleven o'clock. I was ready to attribute their early departure to fatigue from the journey, but it turns out that this is their way. In general, Merezhkovsky is moderate and proper in the extreme. He drinks no more than half a liqueur glass of madeira a day (because he has kidney-trouble) and, when he goes out, puts on under his fur coat his wife's white knitted shawl.

I stayed a little longer. Olga Mikhailovna said to me: "You looked at Zinaida the whole time as if you were madly in love with her." I've heard that several times since, but through no fault of mine.

The next day we all lunched with Polyakov. Again they talked about Christ. "You must admit that Christ is the highest individuality and the highest objectivity. All of the world's past was for his sake, therefore he encompassed all the past in himself, and at the same time he is the highest personality. One must either confess Christ to be the Messiah and then become a Christian, or if not, one must immediately proclaim oneself to be the Messiah. There is no other path."

"Is it really impossible to be saved outside Christianity?"

"It is perhaps possible, but difficult. But if one is against Christ—it is impossible. Look what a plague is hitting the Decadents: Dobrolyubov, Konevskoy, Erlich.[74] It is an omen. I feel that the end to all is near. Now one must either act or perish."

"Yes," Zinochka joined in, "we see that to be saved alone is impossible and we want others to be with us."

Incidentally, she is far from echoing her husband's words all the time. She also chattered womanlike with Polyakov, so that her husband would interrupt, "Don't rattle on, Zina, I'm talking serious things and you break in with silliness!" [. . . .]

In the evening the Merezhkovskys came to visit us. There were, besides, Yurgis and his wife, Polyakov and Durnov, no more. The Merezhkovskys came last. We [Eda and I] awaited them with some trepidation, dressed up the apartment every way we could, turned on the lamps, arranged flowers, got a sofa for Zinochka. Our guests sympathized with our trepidation. Finally the Merezhkovskys came. At first Zinochka talked trivia about how she likes to sleep with an open window and to rush to the bathtub in the morning without dressing, etc. Of course she made two or three jabs. Over tea everyone became a little jollier. Again they talked about Christ, but better than that, they recited poems. Very

---

74. Doubtless refers to Konevskoy's death and Dobrolyubov's disappearance from society and possible madness. Erlich, the latter's follower, died in an insane asylum.

nicely and without being begged, as always, and very simply, Zinochka recited five or six poems. She didn't like Yurgis. She said that at *World of Art* they call him, "Also sprach Baltrushaitis." Of course she made that up herself. D. S. drank half a liqueur glass of malvasia, Zinochka drank three. They had hardly left when we began almost to dance and celebrate because everything had gone well.

The next day, Saturday, we saw them only in the evening, before going to the lecture. I went with Zinochka. We talked in *double-entendres*. There were few people at the lecture, since the Psychological Society for fear of trouble didn't print any announcements.[75] Merezhkovsky spoke well, his eyes sparkling, but less theatrically than Volynsky. In the audience I noticed Princess Trubetskaya, Plaksin, Mintslova, Kursinsky, Savodnik (also Bugaev, Jr., and Petrovsky) and practically all of the members of the Society. No one understood the lecture. [. . . .] Afterwards, we Scorpions wanted to take the Merezhkovskys with us; and the members of the Psychological Society wanted them, too. A compromise was reached through a ridiculous supper in common at the Slavyansky Bazaar.[76] [. . . .]

[Sunday.] In the evening I dined with [the Merezhkovskys] at Mme O.'s, and afterwards, we went

75. Members of the Moscow Psychological Society were for the most part solid members of the intellectual establishment, interested to some extent in new ideas but doubtless careful about lending their backing to a Symbolist poet, even to such a figure as Merezhkovsky.

76. In her essay on Bryusov "The Possessed One" ["Oderžimyj"] (see the Selected Bibliography), Zinaida Gippius describes amusingly what was probably this same supper. Most of those present were solid, graying, bearded professors, among them the father of Andrei Bely, Nikolai Bugaev, who talked all evening about devils, including one who had driven him about in a cab.

as a foursome (the Merezhkovskys, Mme O., and I) to the Art Theatre to see *Uncle Vanya*. Merezhkovsky was horrified at the play's triteness . . . I preached Fet to them; they don't appreciate him.

Zinochka, as if tired of "representing" something, and feeling uncomfortable with her role of refined priestess, was deliberately crude. "I have a stomachache. Don't be shocked. Where we come from it's completely acceptable to say so when your stomach aches." Her darling husband stopped her from eating much: "It's bad for you." "But I want some!"

At the theatre, grimacing like a provincial young lady, she babbled, "Let's stay for the fourth act. I want to hear the cricket. I want the cricket!" But we didn't stay. [. . . .]

1902

January. [. . . .] My stories are getting published in *Russian Bulletin*.[77] [. . . .] I've been going to the Literary-Artistic Circle, listening to unbearably pedestrian papers and unbearably pedestrian discussions at the Tuesday meetings.[78] What a bore . . . [. . . .] They're attacking me fiercely in the *Russian Bulletin* for taking part in the Artistic Circle. The enemy camp. [. . . .] Unexpectedly I had to read a paper at the Artis-

77. In January 1902, *Russian Bulletin* published three Bryusov stories: "Happy New Year" ["S novym sčast'em"], January 1; "The Marble Head" ["Mramornaja golovka"], January 6; "Minuet" ["Menuèt"], January 20. His fiction and other prose continued to find an outlet in this paper.

78. For Bryusov's continuing role in the Literary-Artistic Circle, see the Introduction. Bely writes interestingly on the subject in his autobiographical volume *Beginning of the Century*. See the Selected Bibliography.

tic Circle. I had promised, but supposed that it wouldn't be needed sooner than two weeks from now. Unexpectedly, coming home at four o'clock, I found a telegram asking me to read "tomorrow." What to do? I wrote it in the morning and read it that evening. All the more because during the morning Feigin himself came begging me to do it. It went well enough. There were quite a few friends. Viktorov made furious objections (beforehand he had come up to meet me), Frenkel objected abusively, and Feigin, Kursinsky, and someone else objected in friendly fashion. I likewise made a furious rebuttal. Applause. Mme Krandievskaya came up to thank me.

At Boborykin's reading I was introduced to the venerable relic. During the discussion I wanted to say something, but he was the one who did the talking, and at length. It was Yashchenko who answered him: "You advise writers to organize congresses and syndicates, but the Russian government is hostile to congresses and to writers. Until the regime changes, nothing worthwhile can be achieved." Two days later they arrested Yashchenko, and also Chulkov, but for another reason, in connection with the (rumored) Moscow uprising to be held with all bells ringing and banners unfurled.

Yury Bartenev, having read my story "The Marble Head," sent me as a gift the same little bust which gave me the idea for the story—by Mino da Fiesole . . .[79]

February. Trip to Petersburg. [. . . .] [Tuesday] evening we were at Benois's. I went with Zinochka and preached her a sermon. She had a sore throat and couldn't answer. She was furious. Benois's place is simple, small pictures on the walls. [. . . .] [I

---

79. See note 77. This story later appears in *Earth's Axis* (Moscow: Scorpion, 1907).

talked] with Nouvel and Nurok about the recent poetry of Verhaeren, Vielé-Griffin, Dehmel, Rilke . . . They are well acquainted with them. And later I talked with Somov about painting. Somov is a nice lad. Nouvel is an esthete. Bakst is an esthete with a shade of dandyism. In the main dining room Merezhkovsky was talking about Paul (the Apostle), saying that he doesn't like him, prefers John. But Paul has "such Beauty!" "There is the esthete speaking," remarked Benois. Rozanov spoke against the Gospels, saying that in them no one loves anyone. "On the contrary, all are in love," said Merezhkovsky . . .

Bakst thinks that my face resembles Verlaine's. [. . . .]

Thursday morning we were at the Dobrolyubovs'. Alexander has been accused of sacrilege and *lese-majesté*. At home he also broke up all the icons . . . There's some danger that he might end up at hard labor. Vasily Gippius, father of Vladimir, is trying to have him sent to a settlement. His mother, outraged at this, is trying to save him by putting him in a mental institution.

"Gippius was always Sasha's evil genius," she says . . . [. . . .] Then they called Alexander himself to see me. He came in, or rather, appeared silently and suddenly stood before me. Just the same as ever. His face was full of merriment or joy. He was quietly smiling. His eyes were bright, joyful. He spoke quietly and little. Before answering, he would fold his hands prayerfully, as if meditating or asking instruction from God. He called me "thou" and "brother," spoke intelligently and, of course, completely coherently. Saying good-bye, he kissed me. His mother tells how, when he is alone, he often sings, improvising verses. "If only they could be written down!" she says. "Various literary people" have come to see him, but he refused to see them. He talked with me about an hour; that was exceptionally long . . .

In the evening I went to the Religious-Philosophical Society.[80] [. . . .] Only Merezhkovsky spoke well—passionately, avoiding scholasticism. [. . . .] But most people had come as if to a performance. They argued about theological questions, as if in Byzantium. This is fashionable. I see the attraction of it. Sluchevsky was there and called it shallow. (It was his first visit.) [. . . .]

Went to see Sologub. "He lies in his den and sucks his paw," Zinochka says of him. He looks like a real school inspector. We talked in a reserved manner. I asked him why he didn't participate in the Religious-Philosophical meetings.

"I'm too lazy to ask to join, but I'm very interested." He spoke extremely modestly about his poetry. [. . . .]

February 17–19. Merezhkovsky is in Moscow. Sunday I lunched with the Merezhkovskys at the Slavyansky Bazaar. They talked again with me, about how I am never sincere. Zinochka also said that only very stupid and obtuse people court her. Later we went to their place, because Olga Solovyova was coming. She wasn't feeling quite well and attacked Merezhkovsky furiously. "You pretend that you still have something to

---

80. The Religious-Philosophical Society, established in 1901 in Petersburg, and in which the Merezhkovskys and Filosofov took leading parts, involved both laity and clergy, "with the goal of a lively exchange of thoughts on questions of faith in a historical, philosophical, and social light" (*New Way*, 1903, no. 1, p. 1 of supplement). Bryusov authored various reports on the Society's meetings for *Russian Bulletin* in 1902 and 1903.

say. But you have nothing to say. If someone is really in pain, he doesn't talk so much. Well, if you have something to say, say it." Merezhkovsky refused. "I," he said, "am perhaps chosen as an instrument, a voice. I am someone possessed. All this must be said through me. Perhaps I myself will not be saved, but I will save others . . ."

Rather few came to his lecture—far fewer than to Flekser's . . . [. . . .]

March 15. Balmont was in Moscow. Balmont received permission to go abroad and to pass through Moscow, which he let me know through Lucy Savitskaya. It was decided that he would spend the night at my house. [. . . .] I met him at the station. He came with [his wife] Ekaterina Alekseevna. He was delighted with Moscow, which he hadn't seen for so long. After supper we recited many poems, but it was not too lively. When everyone had left, Balmont insisted that I go out with him. The two of us went to the Hermitage. He ordered English bitters . . .

He absolutely refused to come back to the house. It was already 9:00 A.M. I brought him back with me almost by force, but he had hardly lain down when he got up and ran off . . . Counter to my expectations, he came back about three o'clock. It turned out that he had sent for his mother from Shuya. I went after her, and Balmont stayed at my place . . . I didn't find his mother, returned, and didn't know what to do with him . . . He insisted that he was going to stay in Moscow: "It's all the same to me." Fortunately, his mother arrived at our house, a strong-minded woman and very like him. At first he didn't want even to approach her, but later he broke down in tears and melted.

"Kostya, time to go to the station," she commanded, and Kostya obeyed. At the station Ekaterina Alekseevna met us . . . We put him on the train and he departed. Incidentally, that same train had an accident near Smolensk, but Balmont wasn't injured. "Maybe hell itself preserved him," Kursinsky wrote to me.

Before Balmont's arrival, there was a supper in his honor at Bachmann's, where they read his new book, still in manuscript, *Let Us Be Like the Sun*. [. . . .]

End of March. Polyakov has been ill all this time. I visited him in Taganka and in the hospital. He is diligently studying Persian, and in connection with it, Arabic and Sanskrit. I gave him a present of a dozen Chinese books which I found in the Saturday market in Lent. Some Russian soldiers must have brought them back from a campaign.

Yurgis left for Italy.

Northern Flowers for 1902 has come out. So far, little talk about it. Only Yury Bartenev attacked it—so much so that later he wrote me a letter of apology. [. . . .]

Trip to Italy, May, June[81] (Left May 5, returned July 11.) [. . . .] Venice appealed to me most of all. People there are apart from the normal conditions of human existence and therefore become a little bit "not people." Despite its market hubbub Venice *cannot* become vulgarized. And moreover, it is a superfluous city, even more, a useless one, and in that is its charm. And further, it is a unique city—without noise, without dust. Its division into two parts is excellent: the city for

---

81. A series of travel essays over Bryusov's frequent pseudonym "Aurelius" ["Avrelij"] appeared in *Russian Bulletin* in June, July, and August 1902.

everything dirty, that is the city of the canals; the city for people—that is the streets. Leonardo's dream! Only foreigners and very rich property owners use the gondolas. The average Venetian lives in the street. There was no space for the Venetians to spread, so they went in for depth, for small things, for the miniature. Every detail of this creation of theirs is beautiful, it is precisely the details that are beautiful. Of the artists here, Bellini and Tintoretto have charmed me.

After Venice, even Florence seemed crude and dirty. Of course her galleries are stunning, especially the Uffizi. Milan produced little impression, it is too European—penny-awful. "The Last Supper" looks the same as its reproductions, because all the delicacy of the work has been effaced. We stayed also on the Riviera. It's the same as our Crimea, its only special feature being more luxuriant vegetation. [. . . .]

Returning from Italy I found letters from Pertsov and Zinochka. Pertsov wrote the news that permission has been granted for *New Way*.[82] He had a personal audience with Plehve. ([VB's note:] Pertsov also came to see me before our departure for Italy. [. . . .] Around that time Bugaev also came to see me, recited his poetry, talked about chemistry. He is just about the most interesting person in Russia. Maturity and even senility of mind along with a strange youthfulness. Here's someone to take Konevskoy's place! [. . . .])

September. I attended one meeting of the Artistic Circle where the fate of the Tuesdays was dis-

82. This organ of the Religious-Philosophical Society was published in 1903–1904 by Pertsov, who was later replaced as editor by Filosofov. Bryusov was at first drawn into cooperation but increasingly fell out of sympathy with its management. See note 95.

cussed.[83] Yuzhin presided and in a very parliamentary manner, too. He addressed the gathering just like a demagogue addressing the "people." I was on the extreme left, along with Lyuboschütz and a friend of Andreyev's sister. But we were defeated. The majority put everything into the hands of the directors. Boborykin was there, we exchanged a word.

However, unexpectedly the directors chose me also as a member of the committee. I was at the first meeting. Stupid things were said. I kept silent. Even more stubbornly silent was Leonid Andreyev, whom I saw there for the first time. He has the face of a newspaper shopworker and long hair—which is a provincialism. We were not introduced. I drew a sketch of him. Noticing this, he started posing.

A certain Klara Rosenberg told us about Chulkov and Yashchenko and how they were exiled. Afterwards, I had a letter from Chulkov from the Yakutsk region, very cheerful. He asked me to send him some books. I cling to this corner of that world [of the political exile] to which I have so little access. [. . . .]

October. I have become acquainted with a whole set of new young people. The two Koyranskys—too young, but not without some sort of spark, especially the younger, an artist, who is keener. Pantyukhov, fat, clumsy, but strangely fond of the new poems. Then came Borodaevsky. His poems are rather watery, but as a person he is more interesting, though not much. And then someone named Remizov just in from Vologda. There they are, holed up in Vologda, sending for copies of Ver-

83. On Tuesday evenings a hall in the Literary-Artistic Circle was set aside for events featuring the new art. See the Introduction.

haeren, reading, judging. This Remizov is a rather confused maniac. Suddenly, unexpectedly, for one Wednesday meeting only, Yashchenko appeared from Siberia, also confused. He is swept up by the chaos of events, dreamy, infected by the poison of revolutionary notions, but able to feel and breathe. The most interesting of all these minor ones is of course Alexander Blok, whom I do not know personally. And yet more interesting, though not at all minor but a very major figure, Boris Bugaev, the most interesting man in Russia. [. . . .] In the Artistic Circle the Tuesdays are going on. Idiots utter stupidities, and that's the way the evenings go. The ones who say the more stupid things get the applause. And they go mad from joy if the orator obliquely hits at or spits on the government or Christianity. [. . . .]

November. [. . . .] Baltrushaitis was at Andreyev's on Monday. All the greats were there: Skitalets, Gorky, Shalyapin, Bunin, etc. . . . I saw them all, except Gorky, at the premiere of *The Power of Darkness* . . .[84] Skitalets (Petrov) strode around proudly among the audience. I had very nice conversations there with Sablin and . . . Bazhenov. The latter is more interesting than one would think.

The next day at the Artistic Circle I saw Remizov, my

---

84. Tolstoy's *The Power of Darkness*, written in 1886, was forbidden performance in Russia till 1895, at which time it was produced in both Moscow and Petersburg. The Moscow Art Theatre production was not well-received, Stanislavsky believed, because the spiritual side was not conveyed. Earlier in 1902, Bryusov published his article "Unnecessary Truth. On the Moscow Art Theatre" (*World of Art*, no. 4), in which he argued against the Art Theatre's naturalistic tendency in staging, which he thought detracted from the artist's creative function. As example he cited the cricket to be heard in *Uncle Vanya*. (See Zinaida Gippius's remarks quoted in the final entry for year 1901.)

admirer from Vologda. He has come over to "us" from the extreme Red camp. He had interesting things to say of Berdyaev, Bulgakov and others of his Vologda circle. [. . . .]

November 13. Petersburg. Arrived yesterday. The Merezhkovskys received me like an old friend, as if nothing had happened. "What's all this? You can come in without being announced. Sit down and tell us everything." Incidentally, Zinochka added, "One must behave always so that, even if one knows something, one seems to know nothing." Talked with Zinochka for two hours, dined with them, stayed till twelve, etc., etc.

Pertsov presented me to everyone as the secretary of *New Way*. Obviously they want to force me to accept this as a *fait accompli*. I saw the printing shop, heaps of galley-proofs, and the Literary Bookstore. The editorial office has its cat Maupassant, and oilcloth sofa and a copper nameplate for which the engraver wants thirty-five rubles but which the landlord won't allow them to hang.

"We are all so unfortunate," said Merezhkovsky, "that it's downright touching! Pertsov brings in his miserable three thousand and trembles, we all give all of our work, there are so few of us, we're ridiculous, and there on the other hand are Maxim Gorky, Andreyev . . . It's clear that all we can expect is martyrdom." Merezhkovsky has changed markedly. He abused the "clerics" mercilessly and said that he was an incorrigible "liberal." "Their cause is sacred." (His words.)

November 16. [. . . .] Attended the thirteenth meeting of the Religious-Philosophical Society. Relations have clearly changed. As might be expected, a schism has developed between the church and the laymen. The subject was marriage. Rozanov's paper (read for him, since he was not there because of his wife's illness) raised a storm. Father Mikhail, not understanding it, said that he agreed with Rozanov's critique. Mirolyubov observed that, on the other hand, Rozanov certainly did not agree with Merezhkovsky. Merezhkovsky jumped and shouted that he was not in agreement with Rozanov, but that Rozanov was closer to him and more of a believer than the churchmen. The talk turned to the poem "There lived in the world a poor knight."[85] Merezhkovsky said this was the ideal of sanctity, but Father Mikhail said that it was a Sodomite sin and that Merezhkovsky was preaching the ideals of Stavrogin. Merezhkovsky jumped up again and shouted, "Excuse me, that's really a lie! You can't say such things about a living man." He was almost ready to start an uproar. Skvortsov, Antonin and others filled out the picture. Minsky kept ringing the chairman's bell in vain. [. . . .]

Was at Sluchevsky's Friday gathering. At first everything was decorous. They recited poems—poor ones, of course. I recited "The Crypt" and others. Minsky and Sologub were there. [. . . .] Something monstrous began at supper. After indecent poems by Myatlev, Chernigovets, and Benedikt, they began to tell anecdotes, one more indecent than the other, one more vulgar than the other. Everyone was "dying" of laughter. And it went on and on and on . . . "And here's another one . . ." "And do you know this one." "And here's one . . ." and guffaws, guffaws, guffaws . . . [. . . .]

85. Pushkin's poem "There lived in the world a poor knight" was not published in his lifetime. In its original form, it portrayed a knight whose vision of Mary, the Mother of Jesus, caused him to dedicate himself entirely to her, praying no more to Father, Son, or Holy Spirit.

Was at Minsky's again. They live in a luxurious Venetian palazzo on the English Quay. From the window you can see the Neva. Lyudmila imitates Zinochka, lying on a couch by the fireplace. I recited "The Crypt" for her again. She said some decadent things and flirted in a decadent manner. [. . . .]

November 20. Bakst designed a splendid logo for the journal. The Merezhkovskys like it very much, but Pertsov resolutely rejected it for its "Decadence." "It won't look like *New Way,* but like *World of Art* or *Northern Flowers.*"

Again we had a big argument. Pertsov sent an invitation to Dedlov. We talked about the Last Judgment. Merezhkovsky is convinced that it occurs for everyone immediately after death. For some reason Merezhkovsky begged me to take part in the journal: "If you want, I'll go down on my knees." And he really did. [. . . .]

Went to *World of Art* for the editorial staff's Tuesday meeting.[86] Dmitri Filosofov was there, and Sergei Diaghilev, fat Mr. X., Bakst, and later Nouvel. Semyonov was with me. We talked about the Moscow "World of Art" exhibit, which is causing such a stir in the papers, and whether to discontinue the literary section of *World of Art.* I strongly urged them not to. They asked me to remain a contributor. We argued at length

86. The title "World of Art" refers to a society, a journal, and a series of art exhibits, all devoted to reviving Russian art in much the same way as the Symbolist movement strove to renew Russian letters. It grew out of a schoolboy society, the "Nevsky Pickwickians," reacting against the indigenous "Wanderer" trend and drawn strongly to Western art generally. After several preliminary exhibitions under other titles, the first "World of Art" exhibit was held in 1899, the same year the journal of that name was established. The last exhibit of the series closed in March, 1903, and the journal closed at the end of 1904, thus ending the first stage of "World of Art's" activity, which had tremendous influence on artistic taste in Russia.

about individualism. I liked Diaghilev less than Filosofov; he's too much of a "Sergei-baby." Filosofov is a strikingly "subtle" person. Nonetheless, I can breathe better in the atmosphere of *World of Art* than at the Merezhkovskys. [. . . .]

December in general. We went to see Dobrolyubov. He is in a mental hospital. But even the doctors now agree that he's sane. He told me all about his life during these last few years.

He went away with the intention of preaching the devil and freedom. On the first lap of his journey he met a certain Peter, an uneducated man but one who had figured out everything for himself. He taught Dobrolyubov many things. When Dobrolyubov revealed to him his secret thoughts, Peter was tempted and left him. At Solovetsky Dobrolyubov was drawn in completely. He burned all his books and came to believe in all the rituals. Only on the second trip did he begin to free himself somewhat. The Molokans taught him many things . . .[87] When he was arrested, he was not convicted at the trial. He was only required to sign a statement that he would not leave the area. He lived for a long time in Orenburg, but finally realized that he could no longer stay there. He went to the authorities and declared he was leaving. He left. Two days later he was arrested and sent to Petersburg. At this point Dobrolyubov has returned to the certainties of his early years, that there is

87. The Molokans are a religious sect formed in the later eighteenth century, an offshoot of the Dukhobors (see note 96), subject to much repression for their heresies against the Orthodox Church. In doctrine they are close to Western Protestantism, basing themselves entirely on the Bible. The name refers to the fact that they drink milk during times of fast.

no God, but only the individual personality, that religion is unnecessary, that all which gives strength is good, that both science and art are beautiful. In the summer Dobrolyubov even sent me some kind of manuscript for publication, but I didn't receive it. He read his poems, published by Scorpion, and found that "much in them is true." Dobrolyubov intends to return to the life of the intelligentsia. From all this there remains only experience and the certainty that all "speak the same in various tongues . . ."

Dobrolyubov also told me that initially he was much tried by the "devil of lust." But later that passed. And still later it returned. And he began to ponder it. Why is intercourse with one woman not lechery, but with many it is lechery? For all is one; physicality, the multiplicity of bodies is an illusion. And he came to the conviction that intercourse with many is not a sin. From this point began his disillusion with his own teaching. [. . . .]

Zinochka has lost a great deal and become softer and more boring. She talks about what is divine. It's as if her stinger has been pulled out. [. . . .]

1903

January–February. Petersburg. Stayed in Petersburg three more weeks. *New Way* has gotten on its feet. While I was there, subscriptions rose to 1700. Everyday twenty or thirty new ones. Pertsov has begun to look businesslike. Merezhkovsky is self-assured, though he has hinted that he doesn't like being without honoraria. [. . . .] Have been three times or so at *World of Art*. It's uninteresting. They are quarreling on two fronts—with Merezhkovsky and with Benois, with the religious writers and with the esthetes. Merezhkovsky took terrible offense at Shestov's essay and wrote Filosofov a ten-page letter. The latter answered him, etc., etc. [. . . .]

Went with Joanna Matveevna to see Dobrolyubov. The same sober gospel of love and peace. He recited his new poems and stories for us—they are in the old style, perhaps a little simpler. Was it worth going to the Solovetsky Monastery and off to the Urals in order to return five years later to the same old thing?

Merezhkovsky read *The Lower Depths* and went into ecstasies.[88] "That's the real thing! That was written by *that* one (i.e., the devil), behind his back. Oh, this is very powerful!"

In Petersburg I also met Max Voloshin. A youth from the Crimea. He has lived a long time in Paris, in the Latin Quarter. Poet and artist. He's travelled all the way around the Mediterranean on foot. Talks interestingly about Andorra and the Balearic Islands. He's going to Japan and India to free himself in everything from Europeanism. He had letters of recommendation to everyone, to Merezhkovsky, to Minsky, to me . . . In Petersburg he didn't go over so well, but in Moscow everyone fussed over him for nearly three weeks.

Battle in Moscow—February–March

The battle had already begun before my arrival, with Balmont's lecture in the Literary-Artistic Circle.[89] It went on a whole month. It was a battle for the

---

88. Written by Gorky in 1902, the play premiered at the Moscow Art Theatre in December of that year, but was forbidden in the imperial theatres.

89. On February 3 Balmont delivered a paper on Spanish and English poetry of the sixteenth and seventeenth centuries, entitled "The Sense of Personality in Poetry," and on February 28 he gave a talk on Nekrasov. On March 9 Balmont recited his poetry and on

new art. The allies were the Scorpions and the Gryphons (the new publishing house).[90] Balmont and I were in the lead, being the "venerables" (so the newspapers called us), and after us came a whole hoard of youths thirsting for fame, young Decadents: Gofman, Roslavlev, three Koyranskys, Schick, Sokolov, Khesin . . . and also Voloshin and Bugaev. The battle took place in eight acts: the Evening of New Art, two readings by Balmont in the Circle, a reading in the Circle about Decadents, a reading about Leonid Andreyev, two lectures at the Historical Museum, two readings by Balmont at the Society of Amateurs of Russian Literature and at the "Chat Noir."[91] The Evening of New Art was rather unpleasant for me. I wanted to recite something daring and recited the ballad "The Slave."[92] But the audience didn't appreciate my daring and laughed. True, my admirers, of whom there were many, gave me an ovation, but it is unpleasant to be ridiculed. That was the last of the readings. Whatever was the subject in the Artistic Circle, an argument about the new art would instantly arise

---

March 12 he delivered a lecture, "The Don Juan Type in World Literature." The Evening of New Art was March 4. Bryusov's lecture which closed the "battle" was his "Keys of the Mysteries," a programmatic piece which appeared in the first issue of *The Balance* the following January. A month before the start of the "battle," Bryusov delivered a paper in the Literary-Artistic Circle "Art or Life. On Fet's Poetry," which precipitated a considerable scandal. It was published in *World of Art,* 1903, nos. 1–2, and later in Bryusov's volume of essays *Those Far and Near* [*Dalekie i blizkie*].

90. See Sokolov entry in the Glossary.

91. The "Chat Noir," named for its model on Montmartre, was located in a room of an inexpensive Moscow restaurant. Opened March 3, 1903, it was frequented by artists and literary people. Bryusov's calculation here of the number of acts is not clear.

92. "The Slave" describes in first person the feelings of a slave who has dared raise his eyes to his mistress and, as punishment, is chained to the bed during a night which she spends with another.

during the discussion period. Among those who asked to speak were scores of Decadents. And one after another they would talk about the "great" Balmont and Bryusov, about the sweetness and holiness of sin, about the historic event of the founding in such-and-such a year of the cabaret "Chat Noir," etc. The audience was perplexed, applauded some, hissed at others (Schick especially got the worst of it for his youth and his accent, although what he said was probably most interesting of all). The newspapers abused and criticized the Decadents a lot. There were only a few who spoke up from the other camp, but those behaved dishonestly. The public burst into applause at all the liberal speeches. On the first and second days afterward the newspapers were full of abuse—of the most indecent kind. This continued for over a month. Never before in Moscow has so much been said about the new art and written in the papers (though they brazenly distorted what was said at the meetings). It all ended with my lectures on the new art at the Historical Museum. Not many people came, but they were all our own side and they gave me an ovation—a rather small one. [. . . .]

Paris. April. We spent sixteen days in Paris. Saw everything, i.e., museums, the university, theatres, streets, bistros. We refrained only from climbing the Eiffel Tower, and did not visit the Salon or attend the Opera. Paris was really after my own heart. I was amazed at the lack of Decadence there. It has been, run its course, and disappeared. There isn't even any Art Nouveau. Moscow is a more Decadent city. The theatres here are vile. The Moscow Art Theatre is better than Antoine.[93]

93. The Théâtre Antoine was opened in 1897 by producer-

There were people I knew in Paris. Yashchenko, for example. Through him I got into the whole Russian Parisian Circle. We attended lectures at the Russian School of Higher Studies—a parody of a university. I gave a lecture at the *Association des étudiants russes,* the same lecture I gave in Moscow. The audience was much like that in the Literary Circle, only even more uncultured, even cruder. Objections were in the style of Lyuboschütz. Some kind of "village schoolmasters," as they styled themselves, came crawling out and demanded that I explain to them what Decadence is. There were so many people that the hall wouldn't hold them. They sat, stood, swarmed around, were kept out, and it was stuffy and hot . . . However, afterward only the sympathizers remained. [. . . .]

We also went to see Mme Goldstein (an old lady living in Paris). They also showed me a Redon. I wasn't enchanted. We were also at Onegin's. He showed us in great detail some cigarettes, corks, matches, etc., which had to do with Pushkin, while documents pertaining to him were shown only very fleetingly.

But the most interesting, of course, was Vyacheslav Ivanov. He was lecturing at the Russian School about Dionysus. He's a genuine person, though somewhat too much caught up in his Dionysus. We talked about the techniques of verse, becoming very much absorbed, and were almost run over by a fiacre . . . [. . . .]

End of May. We've settled in a dacha in the Mozhaisk district. I watch squirrels, roam, swim in the

---

theoretician André Antoine, after the failure of his Théâtre Libre (which had produced Tolstoy's *The Power of Darkness* in 1888). Antoine carried the practice of naturalism in the theatre to its extreme. Though he had modified his theories by the time Bryusov visited Paris, the latter found his productions unsatisfactory.

river and in the blue of the sky, and play croquet. No "women" here.[94] I went to Moscow for two days, which I spent entirely with Polyakov. [. . . .]

Bugaev's father died. Polyakov and I went to see him . . . Bely was remarkably fine in the new role of man of affairs . . . I remember once we invited Bely to a restaurant. "Probably you've never even been in a restaurant before," I said to him. He became embarrassed and tried to offer excuses. "It's completely accidental, I assure you": right out of *Brothers Karamazov*. [. . . .]

Autumn. [. . . .] This fall I've had a lot of quarrels with *New Way* about the journal's low literary quality and about their rejection of my politics. Then came the affair of my article on the papacy.[95] It appeared in a completely distorted form so that it made no sense. I wrote a very abusive letter to Zinaida Gippius and Pertsov. They answered (Merezhkovsky, too), in the sweetest fashion possible, that they don't know how it happened, that the censor must have crossed things out. It seems that Egorov is running the journal with an almost free hand . . .

Dobrolyubov came to see me. He spent the summer in Samara province. Now he's on his way to Petersburg.

---

94. Since his wife and probably sisters were with him, Bryusov apparently refers to such entanglements as those with Shesterkina and Vilkina.

95. While Bryusov's participation in *New Way* was important for prestige, his Decadence was a worry to the Merezhkovskys, who sought to neutralize his influence by assigning him to write the journal's political survey and keeping him out of literary decisions. (Significantly only ten of his poems appeared in the journal during its two-year existence.) However, even Bryusov's politics turned out to be an embarrassment. His views were distressingly conservative for a journal aimed at the liberal audience. Bryusov later disclaimed much responsibility for this article ("The Papacy," 1903, no. 8) and others of this type.

Those days when we saw him in Petersburg, he called his temptation. Then he was seduced by doubts, but now he believes. He is again serving God. He speaks self-confidently but meekly. He says "brothers, dear sisters," but sermonizes and constantly warns: "Perhaps my words won't even be comprehensible to you . . ." However, he utters chiefly platitudes and repeats the teachings of the Dukhobors.[96] I said many pointed and bitter things to him.

Before he came to me, he stopped to see Leo Tolstoy and talked with him for two days. Among other things he asked what he, Tolstoy, thinks about personal immortality. Tolstoy replied that he doesn't dare deny it, but is inclined to think that souls return again to the elements.[97] Dobrolyubov said Tolstoy is very deficient in the application of his teaching to life.[98]

96. The Dukhobors practiced a primitive, communal form of Christianity, rejected the Church hierarchy and sacraments, and refused to bear arms. After the 1874 conscription law, service became an individual responsibility and hiring of substitutes was no longer allowed. The Dukhobors suffered increasing repression until a mass exodus to Cyprus and to Canada was arranged in 1899, in which Leo Tolstoy assisted. *Dukhobor* means "spirit-wrestler."

97. In a letter of April 16, 1897, Anton Chekhov reported to a friend on Leo Tolstoy's visit to him in a clinic and their discussion about immortality. Chekhov related: "He recognizes immortality in its Kantian form, assuming that all of us (men and animals) will live on in some principle (such as reason or love), the essence of which is a mystery. But I can only imagine such a principle or force as a shapeless, gelatinous mass; my I, my individuality, my consciousness would merge with this mass—and I feel no need for this kind of immortality, I do not understand it, and Lev Nikolayevich was astonished that I don't." (Letter to Mikhail Menshikov, cited in English from *Anton Chekhov's Life and Thought,* letters translated by Michael Heim in collaboration with Simon Karlinsky; commentary, Simon Karlinsky. [New York: Harper and Row, 1973, pp. 301–302.])

98. Tolstoy had great respect for Dobrolyubov's severely Christian way of life at this stage of his career. He agreed with much of his teaching but did not share his mysticism. This was the first of several

I asked Dobrolyubov what he thinks of Christ. He answered, "About whom are you talking? If you mean the son of Mariam, I know nothing about him . . ."

Andrei Bely

Bugaev has dropped by several times. We talked a great deal. About Christ, of course, the experience of Christ . . . Then about centaurs, silenuses, whether they exist. He told how he went looking for centaurs beyond Novodevichy Monastery, on the other side of the Moscow River. How a unicorn walked about his room . . . The ladies in my family, hearing one of us saying these things seriously and the other seriously listening to him, thought we had taken leave of our senses. Afterward, Andrei Bely sent calling cards around to his acquaintances as if from unicorns, silenuses, etc. Some people laughed, some got angry; but Gregory Rachinsky got frightened and went around Moscow raising a fuss. Bely himself became embarrassed and started assuring people it was a "joke." However, earlier it had been no joke for him, but rather a desire to create an "atmosphere," to behave as if unicorns actually did exist. [. . . .]

My Life. The Years 1904–1907

Foreword

I interrupted my diary at the end of 1903. For 1904, 1905, and 1906 only a few fragmentary notes have survived. It's a pity: those were extremely interesting

---

visits by Dobrolyubov to Tolstoy. On this occasion, Tolstoy took Dobrolyubov for a genuine peasant. In a letter shortly after this visit,

years, years of vivid experience for me. Now I haven't the strength to reconstitute the past—memories have faded and been blurred, fit for a memoir but not a diary. I will make only the most general sketch of what I have lived through and then go directly to the present, to recording today and yesterday.

Valery Bryusov.

April 21, 1907, Easter Eve.

From 1904–1905. For me that was a year of storms, a year of maelstrom.[99] Never have I experienced such passions, such torments, such joys. The greater part of these experiences is embodied in my book of poems *Stephanos*. Some of them went also into the making of the novel *Fiery Angel*. At times I was quite sincerely ready to throw over all my past life and take up a new one, to begin my whole life again. I hardly existed at all, as far as literature is concerned, during that year, if one understands literature in Verlaine's sense. I hardly worked at all: [the play] *Earth* was printed from a rough draft. I broke off relations with almost everyone, including Balmont and the Merezhkovskys. I wasn't seen anywhere. Only my ties with Bely remained, but these were rather the ties of two enemies . . .

I spent the spring of 1905 in Finland on the shores of Lake Saima.[100] "And the rippling's quiet illimitability, / Wafting coolness over me, / Calmed the stormy

---

Dobrolyubov begged Tolstoy to print a statement upholding the principles of poverty and manual labor, which illness prevented Tolstoy from putting into practice at this point.

99. The reference is to his liaison with Nina Petrovskaya (see the Introduction). Some Soviet critics prefer to read this as a reference to the Revolution of 1905.

100. See the section "On Lake Saima" in Bryusov's volume of poems *Stephanos* (1906). See also the Appendix.

rebellion, / Gifted me with peace and tenderness / And sweetly flowed into me."

With autumn, began something like recovery. I found myself again.

The Revolution of 1905

I won't say I wasn't affected by our revolution. Of course I was. But I couldn't stand the compulsory requirement to fall into ecstasies over it and to be indignant with the government, which my associates, except for a very few, demanded of me. In general I can't bear predetermined judgments. I had very serious clashes with many of them. I ended up with the reputation of being "rightist" and, with some, of being one of the Black Hundreds.[101]

I was an eyewitness to the whole Moscow uprising. On the first day, I went out walking and met Nikolai Bazhenov and he led me into the Provincial Council, where we found the Princes Dolgorukov and other future active members of the Cadet party. We watched from the window how they were sawing down telegraph poles and building barricades. Later Bazhenov and I sat in the editorial offices of Scorpion, and I gave him a copy of *Stephanos,* fresh off the press.

The next day I wandered about alone, listened to the gunfire, saw the wounded and killed, and saw the leaders of the revolution, most of whom spoke poor Russian. Ghastly rumors were going around. I didn't believe them

101. The Black Hundreds were rightist squads of activists, fired by ethnic and religious hatreds, who attacked Jews and some liberals and intellectuals. They drew especially from the well-to-do peasantry and the lower middle class in the towns.

and felt convinced from the very beginning that the uprising would fail. Toward the end, everyone became so accustomed to the cannonades that my father, who was playing preference, chalked up the number of shots: 101, 102, 103, 104—200, 201, 202 . . . My brother pretended that he was in on everything, in touch with everyone, but all of his information turned out to be nonsense . . . I wrote a rather long memoir of the uprising, but I don't know whether it was preserved.

Reminiscences

Valery Bryusov, early 1900s (probably 1904).
Courtesy of the Institute of World Literature,
Academy of Sciences, USSR, Moscow.

Illustration by Alberto Martini for the second edition of Bryusov's first collection of short stories, *The Earth's Axis* (1910). Martini illustrated Italian editions of Poe, Baudelaire, Rimbaud, and others.

Bryusov (second from left) with his mother, his wife Joanna, and his father in the family home, probably shortly after his marriage in 1897. Courtesy of the Institute of World Literature, Moscow.

Cover by N. Feofilaktov for the monthly literary journal *The Balance*, no. 7 (1906), edited by Bryusov during much of its existence from 1904 to 1909.

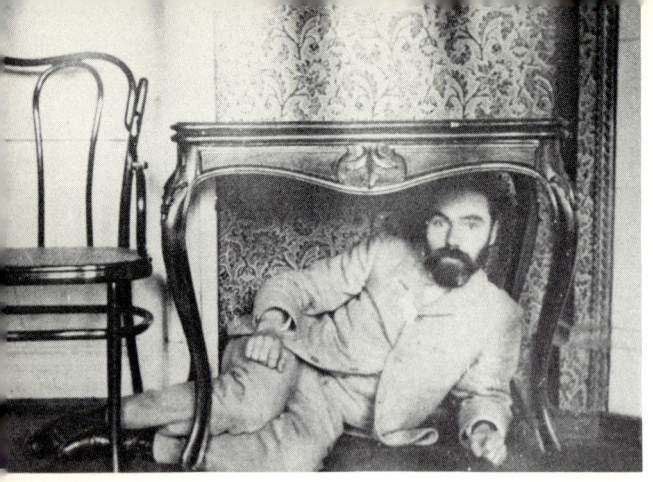

Bryusov under a table, about 1900. From the collection of J. E. Malmstad.

Bryusov with his wife Joanna, about 1913. Courtesy of the Institute of World Literature, Moscow.

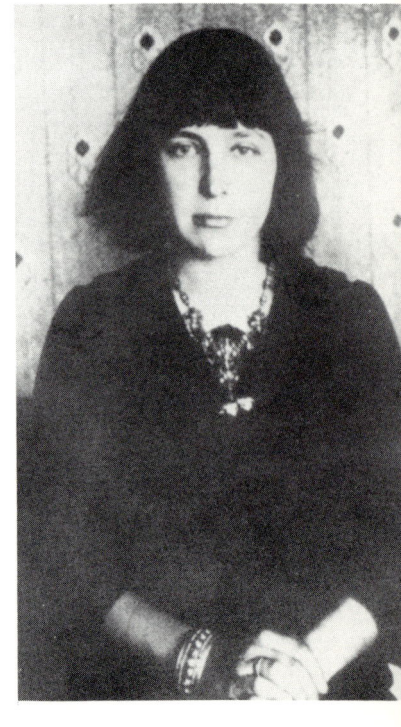

Marina Tsvetaeva (1892–1941), early 1920s.

Oil Portrait of Vladislav Khodasevich (1886–1939)
by his niece Valentina Khodasevich,
first shown in the Exhibit of
Contemporary Russian Painting, 1916.

Bryusov in 1921.
Courtesy of the Institute
of Russian Literature,
Academy of Sciences,
Leningrad.

Photo-portrait of Bryusov, 1923,
by the artist N. A. Bokhanov.
Courtesy of the Institute
of Russian Literature,
Leningrad.

Unfinished charcoal, chalk, and crayon
portrait of Valery Bryusov, 1906,
the last work of the Russian painter
Mikhail Vrubel.

From "Bryusov"
V. F. Khodasevich

When I saw him first, he was twenty-four and I was eleven. I was a classmate of his younger brother. His appearance shook my notion of Decadents. Instead of a naked, shaggy creature with lilac hair and a green nose (this is the way Decadents were pictured in the feuilletons of *News of the Day*), I saw a modest young man with a small mustache, close-cropped hair, a jacket of usual cut, and a cotton collar. Young men like this sold haberdashery on Sretenka. Bryusov is pictured this way in the photograph in the first volume of his works published by Sirin.

KHODASEVICH'S ESSAY "BRYUSOV," from which these passages are taken, appears in Khodasevich's *Necropolis: Recollections*, (Paris: YMCA Press, 1976) (see the Selected Bibliography). Vladislav Khodasevich (1886–1939) began writing poetry under the influence of Symbolism and specifically the Decadent strain cultivated at the time by Bryusov. However, he was soon writing mature, original poetry, and by the time of the Revolution of 1917 was a well-established poet and translator. Khodasevich's reputation as a major poet was made with the publication of *The Way of the Grain* (1920) and *The Heavy Lyre* (1922). He emigrated to Western Europe in 1922 and was soon widely recognized as the leading poet and literary critic of the emigration. This essay was written in December 1924, shortly after Bryusov's death, while Khodasevich was in Sorrento with Gorky. It was first published in *Contemporary Notes*, no. 23 (1925). Later, comparing this piece with Nina Petrovskaya's memoir of Bryusov, Gorky called hers "more humane, though not so brilliant."

Later on, remembering the young Bryusov, I felt that the chief piquancy of his verses of that time consisted just in the combination of Decadent exoticism and the most simple-hearted Moscow bourgeois sensibility. It was an acrid mixture, a sharp disjunction; an acute dissonance, but for this reason Bryusov's early books (up to and including *Tertia Vigilia*) are nonetheless his best books: the most pungent. All that tropical fantasy—on the banks of the Yauza,[1] the trans-evaluation of all values—in the Sretenka district of Moscow. And to this very day I much prefer to the recognized Bryusov that "unknown, mocked, peculiar" author of *Chefs d'oeuvre*. It pleases me that this impudent young man, capable of casually dropping the remark: "I hate my motherland," was at the same time able to pick up a mangy kitten from the street and nurse it back to health in his own pocket while writing his university examinations.

Bryusov's grandfather, Kuzma by name and born a serf, set up a prosperous business in Moscow. He owned a fairly large firm, dealing in fabulous foreign wares: cork. The business was left to his son Aviva, and later passed to Aviva's sons. The sign on their place of business, in a sidestreet between Ilinka and Varvarka, was still intact in the fall of 1920. Almost window to window, but catercorner from that establishment was P. A. Sokolov's notary office. There in the early nineties, on Bryusov's initiative, spiritualist seances were held. I attended one of the last of these, early in 1905. It was dark

1. The river Yauza is a tributary to the Moskva river, joining it in the middle of the city of Moscow. In Bryusov's time, many factories and dye-houses stood on its banks, and as a result its waters were greatly polluted.

and boring. When the group broke up, Bryusov said, "With time, spiritual forces will be thoroughly studied and may even find an application in technology, like steam and electricity." By that time, however, his interest in spiritualism had cooled and I think he had stopped writing for the journal *Rebus*. [. . . .]

There was a time when the famous Wednesdays were held in [Bryusov's] apartment, at which was decided the fate of, if not all Russian, at least Moscow Modernism. In my early youth, I heard of these sessions but dared not even dream of penetrating the inner sanctum. It was only in the autumn of 1904 that I, a newly fledged student, received a written invitation from Bryusov. Taking off my coat in the entry I heard the host's voice, "It is very likely that for every question there are not one but several true answers, perhaps—eight. Insisting on one truth, we run the risk of ignoring the seven others." This idea greatly moved one of the guests, a handsome, blue-eyed university student with fluffy blond hair. When I came into the study, this student was careening about the room with a flying, dancing gait and talking, in rapt excitement, going from a deep bass to the most delicate alto, now almost crouching, now rising on tiptoe. This was Andrei Bely. I saw him that evening for the first time. Another guest, also a student, stocky, rosy-cheeked, dark-haired, was sitting in an armchair with his legs crossed. This turned out to be Sergei Solovyov. There was no other guest: the Wednesdays were by that time in decline.

In the dining room over tea, Bely recited (or more exactly sang) some of his poems. [. . . .] There was at that time something unusually charming in his manner of reciting and in his whole person. After Bely, Solovyov read a poem he had received from Blok: "I wait for death near the morning star." Bryusov condemned the last line severely. Then he himself recited two new poems, "Adam and Eve" and "Orpheus to Eurydice" [*sic*]. And then Sergei Solovyov recited some of his own poems. Bryusov carefully analyzed what was recited for him. His analysis was purely formal. He did not touch on the sense of the poems at all and even seemed to stress that he looked on them all as mere student exercises. This schoolmaster attitude toward such independent poets as Bely and Blok amazed and jarred me.[2] However, as far as I could see Bryusov kept it forever.

Our conversation over tea continued. I noticed that analysis of Bryusov's own poems was not in order. They were to be accepted like the Gospel. Finally, what I was afraid of happened: Bryusov invited me to recite something of mine. Horrified, I refused.

In the nineties Bryusov was leader of the Modernists. Many ranked him lower as a poet than Balmont, Sologub, Blok. However, Balmont, Sologub, Blok were far less men of letters than Bryusov. None of them was so deeply concerned about the *place* he occupied in literature. Bryusov wanted to create a movement and stand at its head. Therefore the formation of a phalanx and the command of it, the burden of battle with opponents, organizational and tactical work—all of that fell chiefly

---

2. In his autobiographical volume *The Beginning of the Century* (see the Bibliography) Andrei Bely describes Bryusov as a severe but devoted teacher of poetry and poets. Bely concludes the passage with an interesting evaluation: "All the talk about his yoke crushing talents is the most arrant nonsense. Occasionally he did make a mistake: at first he didn't include Khodasevich in his list of 'poets'; but he soon rectified his error." (*The Beginning of the Century*, p. 166.)

to Bryusov. He founded Scorpion and *The Balance* and ran them autocratically. He carried on polemics, formed alliances, declared wars, united and separated, reconciled and sowed discord. [. . . .]

The sense of equality was completely alien to Bryusov. Possibly this was due to the influence of the lower middle-class milieu from which he came. It is far easier for the petit bourgeois to bow and scrape before others than, for example, the aristocrat or the worker. On the other hand, the opportunity to lord it over another stirs a lucky bourgeois more than the worker or aristocrat. [. . . .] To show independence meant making Bryusov an enemy forever. The young poet who failed to go to Bryusov for evaluation and approval could be sure that Bryusov would never forgive. Marina Tsvetaeva is an example.[3] Let there spring up a publishing house or journal friendly in spirit but controlled by someone other than Bryusov, and immediately the decree went out that no one published by Scorpion might take part in it. Thus participation in the publishing house Gryphon and later *Art* and *The Turning-Point* [*Pereval*] were strictly forbidden.

Power needs trappings. It breeds obsequiousness. Bryusov tried to surround himself with servility—and, alas, such people were to be found. His appearances were always arranged theatrically. He did not answer yes or no to an invitation, but rather forced people to wait and hope. At the appointed hour he would not be there. Then the members of his entourage would begin to appear. I well remember how once, in 1905, in a certain literary house, the hosts and guests debated for an hour

3. See Marina Tsvetaeva's essay "Hero of Labor," excerpted in this volume.

and a half in whispers: would he come or not? They asked each person as he arrived, "Do you know if Bryusov is coming?" "I saw him yesterday. He said he'd be here." "But this morning he told me that he would be busy." "But at four o'clock today he told me that he would be here." "I saw him at five. He isn't coming." Each one tried to show that he knew Bryusov's plans better than the others, because he was closer to Bryusov. Finally Bryusov would appear. No one dared speak first to him; they only answered if he addressed them.

His exits were equally mysterious: he would disappear suddenly. There was an instance when, leaving Andrei Bely's, he suddenly turned out the light, leaving everyone in darkness. When the lights went on again, Bryusov was no longer in the apartment. The next day Bely received the poem "Loki to Balder," ending:

> But the last ruler of the universe,
> Darkness, darkness is on my side.[4]

[. . . .] He did not like people, because first of all he did not respect them. This was so at least in his mature years. In youth, it seems that he was fond of Konevskoy. His attitude toward Zinaida Gippius was rather decent. There is no one else I could name. His frequently emphasized love for Balmont can hardly be called love. At best it was the amazement of Salieri before Mozart. He loved to call Balmont his brother. Max Voloshin once remarked that the tradition of these fraternal feelings

4. In the poem "Loki to Balder" ["Balderu Loki"], Bryusov polemicizes with Bely, who had treated the battle of light and darkness in his *Northern Symphony*. In his notes to this poem in *Stephanos*, Bryusov gives background from Scandinavian mythology. The lightsome god Balder perishes through the treachery of the evil Loki, and Loki, though he is himself punished, is the ultimate victor.

goes far back in history: to Cain, in fact. In youth he perhaps loved Alexander Dobrolyubov also, but later, when Dobrolyubov devoted himself to Christianity and populism, Bryusov could no longer endure him. Dobrolyubov led the life of a tramp. Sometimes he would come to Moscow and stay with the Bryusovs several days at a time; he had certain religious notions in common with Bryusov's sister Nadezhda. He was a vegetarian, walked around with a staff and called everyone brother and sister. Once I came upon Bryusov at the Literary-Artistic Circle. It was 2:00 A.M. Bryusov was playing *chemin de fer*. I was surprised.

"What else can I do?" said Bryusov. "Right now I'm homeless: Dobrolyubov is staying with us." He wouldn't go home until Dobrolyubov had left.

Boris Sadovskoy, a clever and fine fellow, hiding a very good heart behind a rather dry exterior, was outraged by Bryusov's love lyrics, calling them bedroom poetry. But he was wrong. Bryusov's eroticism is deeply tragic, but not in an ontological sense, as the author liked to think; rather, in the psychological sense. Neither loving nor respecting human beings, he never once truly loved one of those with whom he happened to "share the couch" (to use his poetic phrase). The women in Bryusov's poems are as like one another as two drops of water. This is because there was not one of them he loved, or singled out from the others, or came to know. Possibly he really valued love in itself. But he hardly noticed his mistresses. "Like ministers of the altar we perform a rite . . ." Terrible words because if it is a rite, then it matters not at all with whom it is performed. "Priestess of love" was a favorite phrase of Bryusov's. But a priestess's face is covered; she has no *human* countenance. One priestess may be replaced by another—the "rite" remains the same. And not finding, not being capable of finding, the human person in all these priestesses, Bryusov shrieks with horror, "Trembling, I embrace a corpse!" Moreover, love for him always turned into torture: "Where are we? On a bed of passion / Or on the wheel of death?"

He loved literature, and only literature. He loved himself only in the name of literature. In truth, he fulfilled with holy zeal the precepts which he laid down for himself in his youth: "Do not love, do not give your sympathy, worship yourself alone and without bounds"; and "adore art, and only art, single-heartedly and without other goal." This art for its own sake was his idol, in the worship of which he sacrificed several living people and, it must be acknowledged, himself as well. Literature was for him a merciless divinity, eternally demanding blood-sacrifice. This divinity was embodied for him in a textbook of the history of literature. He was as capable of bowing down to this "building-block of learning" as to the holy stone personifying Mithras. In December of 1903, on his thirtieth birthday, he said to me in so many words: "I want to live so that there will be two lines about me in the history of world literature. And they will be there." [. . . .]

His romance with Nina Petrovskaya was painful for both, but the one who suffered especially was Nina.[5] After completing *Fiery Angel,* he dedicated the book to Nina and in the dedication called her "one who loved much and perished through love." However, he himself had no wish to perish. Having exhausted the plot, in real

---

5. See the Introduction.

life as well as in the literary sense, he wanted to get away to his cozy hearth, to the puffy, well-browned carrot pies, prepared by a solicitous hand and of which he was so fond. With deliberate callousness he made clear his wish to break it off once and for all.

Nina and I were great friends. Moscow gossips assumed that we were more than friends. We laughed a great deal over their assumption and, to tell the truth, sometimes deliberately encouraged the rumors—out of pure mischief. I was aware of and witnessed Nina's suffering and twice spoke to Bryusov about it. During our second talk I said such insulting things to him that apparently he didn't even tell Nina about it. We stopped speaking to each other. However, within six months Nina had smoothed over our quarrel. We pretended nothing had happened.

In the fall of 1911, after a severe illness, Nina decided to leave Moscow once and for all. The day of her departure came—November 9. I went to the Alexandrovsky railroad station. Nina was already seated in her compartment with Bryusov next to her. On the floor stood an open bottle of cognac. (It was the, so to say, national drink of Moscow Symbolism.) They were drinking straight from the bottle, weeping and embracing. In tears, I took a swig also. It was like seeing soldiers off to the front. Nina and Bryusov knew that they were parting *forever*. They finished the bottle. The train started to move. Bryusov and I left the station, got into a sledge and rode silently together as far as the Strastnoy Monastery.

That was at about five o'clock. That day Bryusov's mother was celebrating her nameday. [. . . .] In the evening, after seeing Nina off, I went to her house to congratulate her. I arrived about ten. Everyone was there. Valery's mother was playing preference with him, his wife and his sister Eugenia. Domestic, comfortable, kindly Valery, who had, between the station and the nameday party gotten a haircut and who smelled slightly of hair oil, illuminated by the soft candlelight—said to me, gazing into my eyes with a smile:

"Well, look under what different circumstances we meet now!" I was silent. Then Bryusov, swiftly fanning out his cards as if to say, "Don't you get the joke?" asked pointedly, "And what would you have done in my place, Vladislav Felitsianovich?" The question seemed to refer to the cards, but it had another meaning as well.

I peeked at Bryusov's cards and said, "I think you'd better play low diamonds." And after a moment of silence I added: "And thank God if you get away with it."

"But I think I'll play seven clubs." And he did it. [. . . .]

Bryusov despised democracy. The history of culture, which he worshiped, was for him the history of "creators," demi-gods standing apart from the common herd, despising it, hated by it. Any democratic government seemed to him either a utopia or an ochlocracy, rule by the mob.

Any absolutism seemed to him a constructive force, preserving and creating culture. The poet, consequently, was always on the side of the existing power, whatever it might be—only let it be separated from the people. Like the oarsman of the trireme, it was "all the same, / Whether he drew Caesar or a pirate." All poets were courtiers: in the time of Augustus, of Maecenas, of the Louises, of Frederick, Catherine, Nicholas I, etc. This was one of his favorite ideas. Therefore he was a monarchist under Nicholas II. Therefore, while he still had hope that the Provisional Government would "control the lower classes" and would show itself a "firm power," he tried to get a place on some committees and, trying to support the government's principle of national defense, he wrote and published, in the summer of 1917, a small brochure with a rose-colored cover entitled *How to End the War?*, with the epigraph: "Si vis pacem, para bellum." The idea of the brochure was "war until victory comes." After the October Revolution he fell into despair. [. . . .]

That winter I didn't see Bryusov, but I heard that he was depressed and mourning the inevitable ruin of culture. Only in the summer of 1918, after the dispersal of the Constituent Assembly and the beginning of the terror—he took courage and declared himself a Communist. But this was perfectly consistent, for he saw before him a "strong power," one of the variants of absolutism—and he bowed down before it; it offered him sufficient protection against *demos,* the lower classes, the mob. It cost him nothing to declare himself a Marxist—for it was all the same to him in what name it ruled, as long as there was a power. In Communism he worshiped a new autocracy, which from his point of view was even better than the old one, since the Kremlin was more accessible to him personally than Tsarskoe Selo had been. The old autocracy had had no official policy of patronage toward the arts—the new one wanted to be active in this respect. Bryusov saw the possibility of exerting direct influence on literary matters. He dreamed that the Bolsheviks would offer him the chance to direct literature by firm administrative measures. If that happened, he could command writers without the bother of intrigues and alliances—by a single, barked order. And so many meetings, regulations, resolutions! And what a hope that in the history of literature it would be written: "In such-and-such a year, he turned Russian literature around so-many degrees." Here personal interest corresponded with ideas.

At the end of 1919 I happened to replace him at one of his posts. Glancing into an empty desk drawer, I found there a hypodermic needle and a scrap of newspaper spotted with blood. In his later years he was often ailing—apparently from drug addiction.

Solitary and suffering, he nonetheless experienced an unexpected joy. Toward the very end, he took into his household his wife's small nephew and looked after him as tenderly as he had once looked after the kitten. He would return home, loaded with sweets and toys. Spreading a rug, he would play with the boy on the floor.

Reading the news of Bryusov's death, I thought that he had committed suicide. Perhaps he would have done so at last, if death had not forestalled him.

Sorrento 1924

From "Hero of Labor: Notes on Valery Bryusov"
Marina Tsvetaeva

Translated in Collaboration with Elissa Stern

*"And with secret delight I gaze into
the face of my enemy."* BALMONT

The Poet

From age sixteen to age seventeen I loved Bryusov's poetry with a passionate and short-lived love. In Bryusov I contrived to love the most un-Bryusovian thing. I loved what he lacked in his very core, his very essence—song, the songful element. And this love of mine exists to this day for his *Fiery Angel,* more than for

---

MARINA TSVETAEVA'S ESSAY ON BRYUSOV, from which these passages were taken, was written in the village of Všenora in Czechoslovakia in the summer of 1925. Marina Tsvetaeva (1892–1941) emigrated from the Soviet Union in 1922 and developed into a major poet while in the West, first in Berlin, then Czechoslovakia, then Paris. She returned to the Soviet Union in 1939 and committed suicide in 1941. The lengthy, highly personal essay "Hero of Labor" was undertaken shortly after Bryusov's death in 1924. Tsvetaeva wrote to her Czech friend Anna Tesková that it was a hard task, particularly since all had to be done from memory, without sources. "But perhaps this was better—otherwise a whole volume could have come out of it." I am indebted to my colleague Simon Karlinsky for information on Tsvetaeva gleaned from his book *Marina Cvetaeva: Her Life and Art* (Berkeley and Los Angeles: University of California Press, 1966).

his poetry. I admired *Fiery Angel* then in both conception and execution, now only in conception and the memory of it—in its non-realization. I remember, however, that even at sixteen the word *interesting* on one of those pathetic pages struck me as something vulgar with a price tag on it, inconceivable either in Renata's epoch, in the narrative about the Angel, or in the general pathos of the thing. A master—and such a total miss! Yes, because craftsmanship is not everything. One needs an ear. And Bryusov was tone deaf.

Bryusov's antimusicality, in spite of the extrinsic musicality (in certain places) of a whole series of his poems, reflected the antimusicality of his essence, of his being: dry land, the absence of a river. I remember something that the unique and profound poet Adelaida Gertsyk (recently deceased) said about Max Voloshin and about me, then seventeen. "There is more river in you than shoreline, and in him there is more shore than river." Bryusov was comprised totally of shores—granite ones. [. . . .]

After everything just said, was Bryusov a poet? Yes, but not by the grace of God. A poet, a maker of verse, and, what is more important, maker of the creator in himself. Not the man in the Gospel, who buried his talent in the ground, but a man who by his own will forced it *from* the ground. Something created out of nothing.

"Forward, dream, my faithful ox."[1] Oh, this motto

---

1. "Vpered, mečta, moj vernyj vol!" This famous line is from Bryusov's poem "In Answer" ["V otvet"], first published in *New Way* in 1903 and subsequently in *Urbi et orbi*. Dated August 24, 1902, the poem was dedicated first in draft to Konstantin Balmont and then in *Urbi et orbi* to Peter Pertsov, publisher and editor of *New Way*. It would seem to refer to the pioneering task of those devoted to the new art, and Tsvetaeva may be slightly unfair in quoting the line out of context. See translations in the Appendix.

was no accidental one, it was not inserted for rhyme. It is more like a sigh. If Bryusov was ever truthful to his core, it was in that very sigh. Made out of strength, of sinews, like an ox—what is this, the poet's labor? No, it is his dream! Inspiration plus ox-like labor equals poet. Ox-like labor plus ox-like labor equals Bryusov: the ox dragging the load. This ox is not devoid of majesty. But who else but Bryusov would have thought of likening dream to an ox? [. . . .] If, instead of "dream," he had written "will," the line would have been a formula. A poet of will. [. . . .]

A Letter

[. . . .] I was buying books at Wolf's on Kuznetsky. Rostand's *Chanteclair* was out of stock. At sixteen, not finding the book you want is the same as not finding an expected letter at General Delivery. You wait, were expecting it, and it's not there; you would take it away, but there's nothing. I stood looking for a replacement. But Rostand for a sixteen-year-old is irreplaceable. As he still is for me at certain moments. I stood there, no longer looking for a replacement, when I suddenly heard, behind my left shoulder where your guardian angel is supposed to be, a staccato barking which I'd never heard before, but which I immediately recognized, "*Lettres de Femmes, Fleurs du mal* by Baudelaire, and perhaps *Chanteclair,* though I am not an admirer of Rostand."

I raised my eyes; my heart skipped a beat—it's Bryusov!

There I stood, now having found a replacement, clutching at books, my heart in my throat. For such moments—even now!—I will give my life. And

Bryusov, with his persistent and methodical barking, biting off and spewing out the words "Though I am not an admirer of Rostand."

My heart was in my throat twice over. Bryusov himself! Bryusov of the Black Mass, Bryusov of Renata, Bryusov of Antony![2] And—he is not an admirer of Rostand: Rostand of L'Aiglon, Rostand of Melisande, Rostand—of Romanticism! While I absorbed his final word (which was impossible to absorb, for it expressed the whole soul), Bryusov curtly clicked open the door and went out. I also went out, not to follow him but to meet him by going home and writing him a letter:

Dear Valery Yakovlevich [I am reconstructing this from memory],

Today in Wolf's, while asking the clerk for *Chanteclair,* you said, "Even though I am not an admirer of Rostand." And you said it not once, but twice. Three questions:

First, how could you, a poet, announce your dislike of another poet—to a salesclerk?

Second, how could you, who created Renata, not love Rostand, who created Melisande?

Third, how could you prefer to Rostand, Marcel Prévost? I did not approach you in the bookstore for fear you would construe this as an ambition to "have a chat with Bryusov." You are free not to reply to this letter.

MARINA TSVETAEVA.

I omitted my address so as not to facilitate his reply. (I was at that time a sixth-class gymnasium student, my

---

2. Tsvetaeva prefers the exotic, Decadent image of Bryusov, the creator of Renata. She also apparently admires his poem "Antony" (1905), showing the great Roman warrior casting the world aside to follow Cleopatra's vessel.

first book was to come out only a year later. Bryusov did not know me; but, in all certainty, he knew my father's name, and if he wanted to, he could reply.)

Two days later, if I am not mistaken, a folded note arrived, care of the Rumyantsev Museum, whose director was my father (though we lived in our own home on Trekhprudny Lane). It was not a postcard, that would be too casual. It was not a letter, that would show too much consideration. It was *die goldene Mitte*—the way out of the situation—a folded note. (Typically Bryusovian—"don't overdo it.") I opened it and read: "Dear Madam." (N. B., I addressed him as Valery Yakovlevich in my letter, though he was twenty years older than I!)

I do not remember the opening remarks; there was simply no answer to the poet and the salesclerk question. Marcel Prévost had evaporated. About Rostand he said, word for word, the following:

Rostand is a progressive figure in the movement from the nineteenth to the twentieth century, and a regressive figure in the movement from the twentieth century to our day (this was in 1910).[3] I did not get to love Rostand because it didn't befall me to love him. *For love is fortuitous.* (This last phrase was underlined.)

He wrote a few more words indicating his desire either to meet me or to have further correspondence, but it was

---

3. This incident in fact must have occurred in 1908 or early 1909, if she was indeed sixteen, since she was born in 1892. This is made even more definite by the fact that her father, Ivan Tsvetaev, was still director of the Rumyantsev Museum. In 1909 he was relieved of his post after an accusation that the Symbolist poet Ellis (L. L. Kobylinsky), a friend of Tsvetaev's daughters, had stolen valuable etchings, through Professor Tsvetaev's negligence. Ellis was not convicted, and Tsvetaev was cleared but displaced. Bryusov would have known his name at this time through Ellis.

not explicit, otherwise I would remember. And then the signature.

Naturally I did not reply to the note (for I passionately wanted to).

For love is fortuitous. [. . . .]

Two Little Verses

My first book, *Evening Album,* came out when I was seventeen. It contained poems written when I was fifteen, sixteen, and seventeen. I published it for reasons irrelevant to "literature" but relevant to poetry: in place of a letter to someone with whom I was otherwise unable to communicate.[4] Thus I never became a littérateur; the beginning was portentous.

It was easy to publish a book in those days. Gather the poetry, take it to the typesetter's, select a cover, pay the fee—that was it. This is exactly what I did, a seventh-class gymnasium student, not having told a soul. After the printing, I delivered the lot of five hundred small volumes to the godforsaken bookstore of Spiridonov and Mikhailov (why?) and laid my mind to rest. I did not send out one single copy for review. I did not even know that this was done, but if I had known, I would not have done it. Imagine, fishing for a review! It was impossible to find my book any place but at Spiridonov and

---

4. This first volume of Tsvetaeva's poetry, *Evening Album,* included a number of love poems to Vladimir Nilender, friend of Ellis, whom she considered her fiancé. After the scandal broke (see Tsvetaeva, note 3), Marina was prohibited from any contact with Nilender. Their final break came shortly after the appearance of her book.

Mikhailov. Nevertheless, reviews appeared, and favorable ones at that: a long article by Max Voloshin which marked the beginning of our friendship, an article by Marietta Shaginian (I mention only those that meant something to me), and finally a short notice by Bryusov.[5] This is what stuck in my memory: "Miss Tsvetaeva's poetry is permeated with a kind of terrifying intimacy which at times becomes awkward, just as if one had inadvertently glanced into the window of a stranger's apartment." (I mentally noted: of a house, not an apartment!) The main part, about total mastery of form, the absence of influences, the independence of themes and their manifestation, rare in a beginner: this I will omit, since I do not remember the words. And at the end: "Let us not, however, conceal the fact that there are feelings more poignant and thoughts more necessary than her 'No! The Pharisee's arrogance is repugnant to me!' But when we learn that the author is only seventeen, we are indeed at a loss for words . . ."

Coming from Bryusov, this treatment was unusual. I was, I repeat, congratulated on the review. But out of all the pleasant things, I naturally remembered only the unpleasant; and so I laughed it off: "Thoughts more necessary and feelings more poignant? Just you wait!"

A year later my second book came out, *The Magic Lan-*

---

5. Bryusov's remarks appeared in a review, "New Collections of of Poetry," appearing in *Russian Thought,* 1911, no. 7. Tsvetaeva's memory plays her false. Bryusov in fact withholds judgment on her poetic talent because of her youth but hopes that in future poetry her intimate, domestic images will rise to symbols of general human significance. The flattering judgments which she later "omits" may have come from another reviewer.

tern (1912; then a hiatus till 1922, while I wrote but did not publish). And in it was a verse:

> To Valery Bryusov
>
> Whether you smile into my "window"
> Or number me among the clowns,
> You will not change me, no matter what!
> God has not granted me
> "Poignant feelings" and "necessary thoughts."
> One must sing that all is dark,
> That dreams threaten the world . . .
> —This is the fashion these days.—
> God has not granted me
> These feelings and these thoughts.

In brief, the troops crossed the border. On such-and-such a date in such-and-such a year, I, a nobody, opened warfare on—Bryusov.

It was not exactly a brilliant little poem, but that's not the point. The point was rather Bryusov's response to it.

"Miss Tsvetaeva's second book, *The Magic Lantern*, unfortunately has not lived up to our expectations. There is an excessive, pernicious lightness in her verse . . . ." (Then a series of unpleasant remarks which I do not recall, ending with:) "But what can one expect from a poet who herself admits that God had not granted her poignant feelings and necessary thoughts." The words I had taken from his first review and used in quotation marks now appeared without the quotation marks. I looked like a fool. (See Valery Bryusov, *Those Far and Near*, a book of critical essays.)[6]

---

6. Tsvetaeva is also mistaken here. The review mentioned above (Tsvetaeva, note 5) is reprinted in *Those Far and Near*. The *Magic*

My retort was swift. Almost on the heels of *The Magic Lantern*, I published a short selection from the first two books called accordingly, *From Two Books,* and there, in black and white, I printed:

To Valery Bryusov

I forgot that your heart is only a night lamp,
Not a star! I forgot about that!
And that your poetry comes from books
And your criticism—from envy. A young fogey,
For one instant I mistook you again
For a great poet.

Curiously enough, this poem came to me not after the review, but after a dream about him, with Renata in it, a magic dream of which he was never to learn. The punch of that poem lies in its ending, and if I were Bryusov, I would have paid attention only to the last two words. But Bryusov was a poor reader (of human souls).

This time no response followed in print, but "in the mountains"[7] (of his stark soul), the "response" continued for the rest of his life.

Lantern is mentioned in another review article in *Russian Thought,* 1912, no. 7, "Today in Russian Poetry." Here Bryusov in fact writes as follows:

> Miss Tsvetaeva . . . is true to herself, continuing determinedly to take her themes from the narrowly intimate sphere of personal life, even seeming to boast of this fact ("God has not granted me poignant feelings and necessary thoughts"). . . . Five or six genuinely poetic and beautiful poems are submerged in her book in the waves of purely "album" verses, which can interest, if anyone at all, only her close friends.

7. Presumably a reference to the first words of a sonnet appearing in Bryusov's collection *Experiments* (1918) or to the title of another poem, "In the Mountains," first published in the third volume of his collected works, 1914.

I do not delude myself. In my emotional experience, or more exactly in that youthful experience of enmity, Bryusov meant incomparably more to me than I did to him, in his weary experience. In the first place, for me he was "Bryusov" (a presence to be reckoned with), and he did not like me. For him I was—X, who did not like him, and whose only importance was that I did not like him. I did not like Bryusov, while he did not like one young poet among many, who happened to be a woman, whom in general he despised. I never felt contempt for him, either then, when he was at the height of his fame, or later, when he lay under its ruins. I know this by the emotion with which I now write these lines, that unerring emotion evoked only by grandeur. I challenged him, yes; I was impudent to him, yes; but as for contempt, no. And perhaps I challenged him and was impudent only because I was unable to (did not want to?) express otherwise my very strong feeling of rank. In short, if I were to translate our encounter into school terms, I had been impudent to the principal, the headmaster, not to a mere classroom teacher. There was reverence in my challenge; in his reaction there was only irritation. The importance of the sense of enmity was in direct proportion to the importance of its object. Thus in this nonlove story (since the only gain from any emotion is in experiencing it maximally), the winner was—I.

Revolution—Lito

It was 1919, the most plague-ridden, the blackest, the most deadly of all those years in Moscow. I don't remember who, maybe Khodasevich, suggested that I take a book of poems to Lito [Literary Division of the Commissariat of Education]. "Lito doesn't print anything, but they buy everything." I: "Wonderful." "Bryusov is the head." "Also wonderful, but less so. He can't stand me." "You, but not your poetry; I guarantee he'll buy it. Anyhow—it's five days' bread." [. . . .] I submitted the poetry, and that was the last anyone heard—both of the poems and of me.

About a year passed. I went on living, and the poems lay somewhere. I thought of them with invariable distaste, as of things that had been pawned, not redeemed in time, and now no longer my own. But somehow I pulled myself together and went to Lito. Nothing and nobody: only Budantsev. "I came to find out about two books of poems which I submitted about a year ago." Slight embarrassment; and I, helpfully: "I'd very much like to get the manuscripts back—since, evidently nothing has come of it?" Budantsev, joyfully: "Nothing, nothing. Between us—Valery Yakovlevich is highly against you." "Even slightly would be enough. But the manuscripts—do they still exist?" "Indeed, indeed, I'll get them immediately." "Marvellous. That's more than a poet can expect in our day."[8]

And so I took the manuscripts home. There I opened and leafed through them, and—oh, surprise!—the second autograph of Bryusov I had received in my life! Three whole lines of comment—in his hand!

"M. Tsvetaeva's verses, since they were not published at the proper time and do not appropriately reflect the contemporary period, are useless." No, there was something else; I've remembered, as always, the high point, the end. I have a visual impression of three lines of

---

8. Tsvetaeva's *Versty I* was subsequently accepted by the State Publishing House and appeared in 1922.

Bryusov's cramped, stingy, careful handwriting. What could have been in the other line and a half? I don't know, but there was nothing worse. [. . . .]

Later, when I ran into Budantsev, he pleaded fervently and touchingly for me to return the comments. "You weren't supposed to read them. That was my oversight; I'll be blamed for it!"

"Oh, but really, this is my *titre de noblesse,* my patent of nobility like Tyutchev's, my privileged ticket anywhere where poetry is honored!"

"Copy them and return the originals!"

"What do you mean! I should give back Bryusov's autograph? Autograph of the author of *Fiery Angel?* (A pause.) Give it back when there is the chance of selling it? I'm going abroad and I'll sell it there, tell that to Bryusov!"

"And Bobrov's comments? [The second reader.] At least give back Bobrov's!"

"And I'll sell Bobrov's for good measure. Three lines of Bryusov's—so much, and I'll throw in four pages of Bobrov. Tell Bobrov that."

So I made a joke of it, but didn't give in.

[. . . .] I might have loved Bryusov, if not just like any other poet—Bryusov is manifested not in his poetry but in his will to poetry—then like any other form of strength. And having strained my discernment to the utmost, I affirm: under the sincere guise of hatred I simply loved Bryusov, only more strongly in that aspect of love (repulsion) than I would have loved him in the simpler guise—attraction.

Bryusov, who was emotionally deaf, did not sense that, and purely and simply could not bear, at first the "chit of a girl," later the "woman," the whole sense and meaning of whom—I insist—was in love and not in hate, in the hymn, not the epigram.

If Bryusov, from the heights of his low Roman skies, from the depths of his lofty Gothic underworld, hears this, I will hear the sound of his name with less pain.

[. . . .] Bryusov will appear in the anthologies, but not in the section "Lyrics." He will be found in that section—and there will be such a section in Soviet anthologies—"Will." In that section (of builders, conquerors, overcomers), his name, I want to believe, will be among the first of Russian names. And my heart, unjust but thirsting for justice, will not rest until there is in Moscow, in its most prominent square, a granite statue larger than life, with the inscription: To a Hero of Labor of the USSR.

Appendix:
Twenty-One Poems by Valery Bryusov

Translator's Note

These poems were chosen from volumes Bryusov published between the years 1895 and 1912. The texts used are found in the *Collected Works* (Moscow, 1973–1975). The selections are not necessarily the *best* poems he ever wrote, but they include a number that made him famous. I have aimed at a representative selection illustrating various styles and themes found in his work. The translations strive for fidelity to meaning and mood rather than to verbal structure. Bryusov normally wrote stanzaic rather than free verse and is noted for his innovative practices in rhythm and rhyme. I have preserved stanza form but have not attempted to duplicate either rhythm or rhyme scheme, feeling that, as Tolstoy said of *Anna Karenina,* the only way to convey the totality of the work is to write it all over again. And in Russian. I hasten to add that my practice does not reflect Bryusov's theory of translation, which was much more ambitious. But Bryusov was also a poet.

Premonition

My love is the torrid noon of Java;
A fatal aroma wafts about like a dream,
There pangolins lie, their pupils veiled,
Here boas twine the trunks of trees.

And did you enter this inexorable garden
For amusement, for sensuous play?
Flowers tremble, grasses smell more pungent,
Everything enchants, everything exhales poison.

Let us go: I am here! We will take our pleasure—
Frolic, wander in wreathes of orchids,
Entwine our bodies, like a pair of greedy serpents.

Day will slide by. Your eyes will close.
That will be death. And in a shroud of lianas
I will wrap your motionless form.

25 November 1894

"Predčuvstvie" from *Chefs d'oeuvre* (1895)

To a Young Poet

Pale youth with burning gaze,
I give you now three commandments:
Accept the first of them: live not in the present,
Only the future is the poet's realm.

Remember the second one: sympathize with no one,
Love only yourself without limit.
Observe the third one: worship art,
Only art, unfalteringly, without reckoning.

Pale youth with troubled gaze!
If you accept my three commands,
I shall fall silently, a conquered warrior,
Knowing that in the world I have left a poet.

15 July 1896

"Junomu poètu" from *Me eum esse* (1897)

A Painful Gift

*I soar, a winged sigh,
Between earth and heaven.*
E. BARATYNSKY

A painful gift the gods have given me,
Having placed me on a mysterious boundary.
Thus I wander in insane alarm,
Thus am I tormented by painful expectations.

I hear the sounds of another world,
The steps of eumenides, the prophecies of lamias,
But in vain I stretch out my hands in supplication,
Walls stand invisibly between us.

The earth is alien to me, the heavens inaccessible,
Dreams forever, forever impossible.
My desires are criminal before the world,
Before heaven my inspirations are insignificant!

25 October 1895

"Mučitel'nyj dar" from *Me eum esse* (1897)

There is something shameful in nature's power,
A dumb enmity toward beauty's rays:
The years drift over the world of crags,
But only the world of dream is eternal.

Let the changeless ocean threaten,
Let the icy ridges proudly sleep on:
A final day will come for the universe,
And only the world of dream is eternal.

July 1896
The Crimea

> "Est' čto-to pozornoe v mošči prirody" from *Me eum esse* (1897)

Psyche

What did you feel, Psyche, on that day
When Eros led you as his bride
To the gods' feast in otherworldly halls?
What did you feel in their Olympian circle?

Could all the love of him who is the god of love
Relieve the barely concealed hurts:
Ares' insolent glance, the queen's wrathful sigh,
Whispers of goddesses and Aphrodite's malicious
    greeting!

And at the gods' feast, hearing their shameless laughter,
Where all are above the law—gods and goddesses,
Did you not recall the days of earthly joys,
Where there is sadness and shame,
    where there is faith in what is sacred!

23 December 1898

    From *Tertia Vigilia* (1900)

Cassandra

Cassandra, prophetess!—your shade,
Having passed on to blessed Lethe,
Found not the consolation of nonbeing;
Here too your dreams burn with the flame of centuries.

Your spirit lives in visions of better days,
In thought you are there, near Ida, by Skamander,
You seek the circle of kindred shades,
You sing to them in Hades, prophetess Cassandra!

You call the chieftains and,
　　　once more full of Phoebus' gift,
Vengeance you praise, aflame with hope—
That the Achaean tribe will suffer vengeance,
Thrown into the dust by the offspring of Aeneas!

But Lethe's moisture has quenched all their thirst,
And vainly you strive to wake their desire for revenge!
The laughter of beyond the grave twists the heroes' lips:
You exalt—and all is still, you call—and no one answers.

8 March 1898

From *Tertia Vigilia* (1900)

Moses

As I returned from the secret heights to my people
Great words rang in my dreams.
I believed that they waited and hoped . . .
They, forgetting me, danced about the calf.

Gazing on that festival, I understood them. And so
I dashed the useless tablets on the rock
And cursed forever Thy chosen people.
Yet in my heart was neither wrath nor grief.

But Thou, O Lord, hast commanded me again
To carve out tablets. For the guilty mob
Thou hast left Thy law. So be it. Love

I dare not judge. But to me, to me it is
Inaccessible. What Thou hast commanded, I do,
But as everlasting as love—is my scorn.

25 April 1898

    From *Tertia Vigilia* (1900)

I love big houses
And narrow city streets—
On days when winter is not yet,
But autumn already wafts cold.

The expanse of squares I love,
Protected by walls all around,
In the hour when streetlamps are not yet lit,
But shy stars begin to gleam.

I love the city and its stones,
Its rumble and its singing sounds,
In the instant when I hide a song deep within me,
Yet in ecstasy hear its harmonies.

29 August 1898

"Ja ljublju bol'šie doma" from *Tertia Vigilia* (1900)

Struggling with spring, the winter cold grows sparse,
The web of wires more free and soft,
The snow, grown dark, heaped up, is cleared,
The street's recess is filled with shadows.

Far off and near—all speaks to me of change:
The flocks of birds that circle round a cross,
A ringing stream that rushes by in foam—
And this woman here, with her enormous belly.

25 February 1899

> "V bor'be c vesnoj redeet zimnij xolod" from *Tertia Vigilia* (1900)

Demons of Dust

    There are demons of dust,
As there are demons of snow and of light.
    There are demons of dust!
Their garments of crimson hue
    Burn like flame.
    But with ironical smiles
They cover them with a gray cloak.

    Demons of dust
Hide in cupboards like beasts
    And close their eyes.
Yet hardly are the doors thrown open,
    But they tremble
    And look about wildly;
They shoot up and reel about, do the demons of dust.

    Where they have conquered,
There is quiet, there is sleep and dreaming,
    As in a spacious tomb.
They drowse, lie motionless,
    Concealed in a corner,
    Not gazing into the darkness,
But recalling in their sleep that they have conquered.

O demons of dust!
You are sovereigns in the colorful world!
O demons of dust!
Your power grows vaster with ages!
Your day will come—
All will fall asleep
Beneath the quiet drift of your gray soaring.

21 February 1899

"Demony pyli" from *Tertia Vigilia* (1900)

The Ultimate Desire

Where shall I realize and quench
My ultimate desire?
Shall I find that unthinkable knowledge,
Which secretly I love?

Shall I go to the solitary hermitage,
Golden-domed in the forest,
And to a cell bring my uncooled fever
Before the nighttime vigil lamp?

Or, in the city, where walls press in,
In hours of mad barricade fighting,
When Dream and Riot rule,
Shall I gladly merge with life?

Or, once for all embracing books,
Intoxicated with the dreams of all ages,
Shall I yield myself to you—O moments—
Inexhaustible, sonorous revery?

I have allied myself with diverse forces,
Borne alien banners,
And here again, like a thirsting prisoner,
I look on freedom from a window.

January 1902

"Poslednie želanie" from *Urbi et orbi* (1903)

In Reply

TO P. P. PERTSOV

Long enough have I, patient ploughman,
Guided my heavy plough.
    A. KHOMYAKOV

A long while yet I shall roam
The furrows of this earthly field,
A long while before I release
This tired ox from the plough.

Onward, dream, my faithful ox!
I'll force you, if you are not willing!
I am beside you, my whip is heavy,
I labor, and you too must work!

Not for an instant may we rest;
Break up the huge chunks of dry earth!
The day is short, the way is long,
Plod on, plod on from turn to turn!

Already noon. The heat burns stronger.
The shadow will not cool us soon.
Empty is the fields' horizon.
No one will greet us: "God succour you!"

But remember how we set out
To the field in the fresh spring morning
And hoped to sing till the sweet dusk,
With others next to us in freedom?

Forget that morning dew,
Do not think of night's repose!
Follow the burning furrow,
My faithful ox—we are only two!

Our task was set by One on high,
Who shall imperatively demand account.
Labor before the mist comes down,
See, our work is just begun!

And in the hour when darkness
Will hide the boundaries of this sphere,
Not I, but that Other, O my dream,
Will free you from the plough!

24 August 1902

"V otvet" from *Urbi et orbi* (1903)

Sonnet

O, skillful dramatist, fate, I cry out "Bravo"
To that effective scene where I am slain.
How cunningly contrived and true to life.
The end is unexpected, but inevitable.

Admit it, I too have played my role to the hilt,
Will they not shout "Encore" to me as well?
But I, having closed my eyes, lie in bloody murk.
I will not answer them, I have been dealt a deathly blow.

I love the beauty of unexpected defeats,
My own demise I praise and sing.
It does not matter whether you or I am onstage.

"All life's a game." I'm wise and this admit.
Stretched in the dust, I have but one desire,
To learn how the fifth act will unwind from the fourth.

4 July 1901

From *Urbi et orbi* (1903)

Fog

Along the quiet canal
Willows bend their boughs.
The road clings to the water,
But the shadows hurry,
And hark! a bird of night
Shrieks a greeting to a star.

Along the quiet canal
Passes a procession
Of white maidens, drooping.
They go wearily,
Their faces veiled,
Their forms wrapped in bridal veils.

From the quiet canal,
Like great white hulks,
Rise rows of horses,
And their riders, glad
To breathe the evening damp,
Hurry faster and faster!

Along the quiet canal
They fly, a dashing band,
And lure the maidens,
Stretch out their hands to them—
And the white cloaks twine
With the white bridal veils!

1903

"Tuman" from *Stephanos* (1906)

Me, who sought madness,
Me, who begged for alarms,
Me, who trusted in revery
To the hum of wheels, in the great city's noise,
Fate has abandoned on a quiet shore.

And the rippling's quiet illimitability
Wafting coolness over me,
Calmed the stormy rebellion,
Gifted me with peace and tenderness
And sweetly flowed into me.

And amidst the thin-stemmed pines,
On a background of blue mystery,
Like a summons from all the longings of this world,
A pledge of wordless confessions—
Your image has risen over me!

1905
Rauha

> "Menja, iskavšego bezumij" from the cycle "On Saima," *Stephanos* (1906)

Yellow silk, with yellow silk
On sky-blue satin
Unseen hands sew.
To the golden horizon
The sun, a flame-bright fragment,
Sinks at the hour of parting.

Someone drapes the distance
With a festive purple fabric,
Spreading the crimson hanging,
And in the yellow-azure water
Fiery-red birds
Dash about glistening.

But silver snakes,
Their backs' shining zigzags
Twisting beneath the radiance,
With merciless lips
Catch and, ever bolder, catch
The birds flickering in the water.

1905
Rauha

"Želtym šelkom, želtym šelkom" from the cycle "On Saima," *Stephanos* (1906)

Adam and Eve

Eve

Adam! Adam! press nearer,
Cling to me, Adam! Adam!
The boughs droop lower, lower,
The fruit bends to our mouths.

Adam

Press nearer, Eva! Eva!
It is dark. Whence this darkness?
Boughs droop from right, from left,
The fruit plunges into our mouths.

Eve

Adam! Adam! Who bends these boughs?
Who bends me, so feeble?
My body sinks in singing waves,
Your touch is of fire!

Adam

What burns my breath, Eva! Eva!
Barely can I glance, or gasp . . .
What is this: fruit fallen from the tree,
Or your living breast?

>Eve

Adam! Adam! All of me is without will . . .
Where are you, where am I? Is this dream or waking?
Adam! Adam! This hurts me, hurts me!
Let me go—oh, cease! cease!

>Adam

So it must be, Eva! Eva!
I am yours! Yours! Be silent! Silent!
Oh, how through the branches from right, from left,
The sun's rays pour in torrents!

>Eve

Adam! Adam! The light shames me!
What have you done? What has happened to me?
You forgot the words of the commandment!
Leave me! Leave me! Let me be!

>Adam

How did I tear off the fruit, Eva, Eva?
How could I crush it so?
Oh, there is the sign of Holy Wrath—
The flowing red, red juice.

January 1905

>From *Stephanos* (1906)

Orpheus and Eurydice

Orpheus
I hear, I hear your gentle steps,
I hear your steps behind me.
We follow a troublous path,
A barren path to life.

Eurydice
You lead, I shall submit,
I must go, I must . . .
But before my gaze is a black cloud,
The shroud of black death.

Orpheus
Upward! Upward! Every step we climb
Leads toward sounds, light, to the sun!
There the shadows will melt from your sight,
There, where my love waits!

Eurydice
I dare not, I dare not,
My spouse, my friend, my brother!
I but drift like a light shadow,
You lead back but a shade.

Orpheus
Trust me! Trust me! At the threshold,
Like me you will greet the spring!
I, having invoked God with my lyre,
Will breathe life into you with song!

Eurydice
Ah, what do melodies mean
To those who have known the mystery of quiet!
What is spring, to one who has seen the sowing
In the land of asphodels!

Orpheus
Remember, remember! the green meadow,
The joy of songs, the joy of dancing!
Remember, at night the hidden
Sweet-burning terror of caress!

Eurydice
My heart is dead, my breast unmoved.
What can I give to an embrace?
I remember dreams, but I cannot grasp,
My poor friend, your words.

Orpheus
You do not remember! You have forgotten!
Ah, I remember every instant!
No, not even the tomb
Can blot out your face for me!

Eurydice
I remember happiness, my poor friend,
And love, like a quiet dream . . .
But in darkness, in darkness without trace
Your pale countenance is lost to me . . .

Orpheus
—Then look!—And Orpheus peers wildly
Back into empty darkness.
—Eurydice! Eurydice!—
Groan the echoes of the shades.

1903, 10–11 June 1904

From *Stephanos* (1906)

To a Dear One

How passionately you awaited an answer!
And I brought you my gift:
My sacred gift, my poet's gift—
A crown of dark-red roses.

My flowers are fragrant,
The rims of their petals flame,
But one crowned with roses knows
The secret stabbing of thorns.

The crown will never fade
Above the brow's quiet aspect,
But every evening again
The hidden needle will wound you.

In this garland, as at a merry feast—
You are a martyr on the cross!
But be faithful in a faithless world
To your ecstatic dream!

My gift is sacred, my gift is the poet's gift.
It has raised you higher than all.
Be proud, as of a wondrous halo of light,
Of this crown of dark-red roses!

11 January 1908

"Blizkoj" from *All Melodies* (*Vse napevy* [1909])

How Many Times

Again it's spring. The familiar circle
Is closed—how many times!
And again the spring meadow is green,
And the evening hour is dewy.

I gaze, as the moon gazes into a dark pond,
Into the pupils of beloved eyes,
Lips press trembling to lips . . .
They press—how many times!

And the instant shall, like a long dream,
Rock us and lull us.
I am strangely happy, I am in love . . .
In love! How many times?

And in graceful strophes once again dreams
Sing—how many times!
And the moon looks down from the heights,
The cold eye of the ages.

February 1907

"Kotoryj raz" from *All Melodies* (*Vse napevy* [1909])

My soul, you are a withered flower!
We are alone again, you and I.

An ocean fish out on the sand.
Mouth open in deathly anguish.

You can writhe but you cannot breathe . . .
Over the quiet sea is heavenly peace.

Over the sea is emptiness:
No smoke, no sail, no cross.

Sunlight reflected in the waves—
The sun's ray does not reach the bottom.

The sun's ray is merciless and scorching . . .
There's not a cloud, never was and shall never be.

Merciless and scorching is the sand in the sun.
The fish has not long to suffer.

My soul, you are a withered flower!
We are alone again, you and I.

[1911]

> "Cvetok zasoxšij . . ." from *Mirror of Shadows* (*Zerkalo tenej* [1912])

Glossary of Proper Names

AKSAKOV, KONSTANTIN (1817–1860). One of the younger Slavophiles (see Khomyakov), noted for interest in external features of early Russian culture.

ALLEGRO (POLIKSENA SOLOVYOVA, 1867–1924). Poet, daughter of historian Sergei Solovyov, sister of philosopher and poet Vladimir.

ANDREEVSKY, SERGEI (1848–1919). Poet, lawyer, and prominent critic. His poetry was pre-Symbolist in theme.

ANDREYEV, LEONID (1871–1919). Modernist writer, began his career in 1898, encouraged by Gorky, and was extremely popular for many years in Russia and abroad.

ANTONIN, BISHOP. Censor for religious and spiritual writings in Petersburg.

Art [*Iskusstvo*]. Moscow, 1905. Monthly of art and art criticism.

Artist [*Artist*]. Moscow, 1889–1895. Theatrical, musical, and artistic journal; seven times a year.

BACHMANN, GEORG (1852–1907). Poet in German and Russian, little published but highly respected by a small circle, some of whom—Bryusov, Balmont, Baltrushaitis—visited his Saturday salons.

BAKST, LEON (LEV ROZENBERG, 1866–1925). Artist of "World of Art" group, noted for exotic stage design for the Ballet Russe and other productions. Adopted his grandfather's name professionally.

Balance, The [*Vesy*]. Moscow, 1904–1909. Journal of literary and art criticism, after 1905 included works of literature. Prestigious organ of Symbolist movement; *de facto* editor was Bryusov.

BALMONT, EKATERINA. Balmont's second wife, whom he married in 1896.

BALMONT, KONSTANTIN (1867–1942). One of the leading Symbolist-Decadents of the older generation. Translated works of Blake, Byron, Poe, Shelley, Baudelaire, Calderón, Verlaine, Strindberg, and others.

BALTRUSHAITIS, YURGIS (1873–1944). Lithuanian Symbolist, translator, poet, wrote also in Russian. Collaborated closely with Bryusov in numerous projects.

Banner [*Znamja*]. Moscow, 1899, 1901. Political, scientific, and literary weekly.

BARATYNSKY, EVGENY (1800–1844). Philosophical poet, next to Pushkin the most important poet of the 1820s.

BARTENEV, PETER (1829–1912). Publisher and editor of the historical journal *Russian Archive* from 1863. Bibliographer and Pushkin scholar.

BARTENEV, YURY (1866–1934). Son of Peter, member of Moscow censorship committee.

BAZHENOV, NIKOLAI (1857–1925). Psychiatrist active in literary affairs, notably Literary-Artistic Circle, author of *Psychiatric Essays on Literary and Social Themes* (Moscow, 1903).

BELY, ANDREI (BORIS BUGAEV, 1880–1934). Major poet, novelist and critic among younger generation Symbolists. Complex figure who expressed the most extreme features of the Symbolist mentality. His relationship with Bryusov held for a time the character of student with master, though Bely was the greater writer.

BENEDIKT (N. N. VENTTSEL). Satirical poet.

BENOIS, ALEXANDER (1870–1960). Founder of Nevsky Pickwickians, student group out of which grew "World of Art," in which Benois was also a leading figure.

BERDYAEV, NIKOLAI (1874–1948). Religious philosopher, prominent figure in history of Russian thought. Evolved from Marxism to strict Russian Orthodoxy.

BILIBIN, IVAN (1876–1942). Artist noted for his illustration of Russian fairytales.

BLOK, ALEXANDER (1880–1921). One of the greatest twentieth-century Russian poets, belonged to younger generation Symbolists. He considered Bryusov and Vladimir Solovyov the greatest influences on his work.

BOBORYKIN, PETER (1836–1921). Minor but prolific novelist and dramatist, recorder of social phenomena in style of French naturalism.

BOBROV, SERGEI (b. 1899). Futurist poet and theorist, showing influence of Symbolism; later, novelist and translator.

BORODAEVSKY, VALERIAN. Minor poet, whose talent was admired by Vyacheslav Ivanov but not by Bryusov.

BRYUSOV, ALEXANDER (1887–1966). Younger brother of Valery, later a poet, translator, and archaeologist.

BRYUSOVA, JOANNA RUNT (1876–1965). Wife of Valery; of Czech extraction. Later editor of some of his works, organizer of Bryusov archive.

BRYUSOVA, NADEZHDA (NADYA). Sister of Valery, his closest companion, a gifted musician and later professor at Moscow Conservatory; at one time attracted to Dobrolyubovians. *See* Dobrolyubov.

BUDANTSEV, SERGEI (1896–1939). Soviet novelist and playwright of somewhat unorthodox type.

BUGAEV, BORIS. *See* Bely.

BUGAEV, NIKOLAI (1837–1903). Mathematician, Dean of the Faculty of Science at Moscow University, father of Andrei Bely.

BULGAKOV, SERGEI (1871–1944). Philosopher, evolved like Berdyaev, from Marxism to Orthodoxy and became priest and theologian.

BUNIN, IVAN (1870–1953). Novelist, poet, translator, winner of the Pushkin Prize for poetry in 1901 and the Nobel Prize for literature in 1933.

BURENIN, VIKTOR (1841–1926). Playwright and literary critic for the reactionary newspaper *New Times,* consistently the most abusive commentator on the new art.

CHEKHOV, ANTON (1860–1904). With Gorky and Tolstoy, one of the leading Russian writers of the turn of the century. Despite some critics' penchant for speaking of his "symbolist" plays, he never came close to the Symbolist camp.

CHERNOGUBOV, NIKOLAI. Moscow antiquarian and collector of literary materials pertaining to Russian writers.

CHIRIKOV, EVGENY (1864–1932). Writer, dramatist.

CHULKOV, GEORGY (1879–1939). Poet, belletrist, and theorist of a brand of Symbolism which he called "mystical anarchism."

CHYUMINA, OLGA (1864–1909). Poetess and translator from English and French; her poetry belonged in style and quality to the 1880s.

Courier [*Kur'er*]. Moscow, 1897–1904. Daily covering politics, literature and social life. Closed by government for sympathetic attitude toward revolutionary movement.

DEDLOV, V. (VLADIMIR KIGN, 1856–1908). Contributor to liberal journals, author of fiction and a study on Chekhov.

DERZHAVIN, G. R. (1743–1816). Outstanding Russian poet of time of Catherine the Great; highly original author of lyrics, odes, anacreontic verse; subject of biography by Khodasevich.

DIAGHILEV, SERGEI (1872–1929). Editor of *World of Art*, organizer of art exhibits under auspices of "World of Art" society, later producer of Ballet Russe.

DOBROLYUBOV, ALEXANDER (1876–1944?). Poet who, in his early years, represented extreme Decadence, demonism. Converted to religious asceticism, he later formed a sect of Dobrolyubovians based on Christian anarchism.

DOLGORUKOV, PRINCES PETER and PAUL. Members of old Moscow princely family, active in the Kadet Party.

DOSEKIN, N. V. Painter of Wanderer group (*See* Diary, note 47), who later joined "World of Art."

DOSTOEVSKY, FYODOR (1821–1881). Among great Russian novelists, the Symbolists' favorite.

DURNOV, MODEST. Poet, artist, architect. Bryusov dedicated verses to him in *Tertia Vigilia*. Balmont dedicated to him the first edition of *Let Us Be Like the Sun*.

EDA. *See* Bryusova, Joanna.

EGOROV, EFIM. Writer for newspaper *New Times,* secretary of *New Way* after Bryusov.

ERLICH, YAKOV (1874–1925). Musician, philosopher, friend of Dobrolyubov; died in an insane asylum.

ERMILOV, VLADIMIR. Teacher and journalist.

FEIGIN, YAKOV. Editor-publisher of the Moscow daily *Courier*.

FET, AFANASY (1820–1892). A major lyric poet of the second half of the nineteenth century. Returning to publication after a twenty-year silence, he enjoyed popularity among the Symbolists.

FIDLER, FYODOR (FRIEDRICH FIEDLER). Teacher of German in Petersburg, translator of Russian poets into German.

FILIPPOV, N. D. Son of wealthy Moscow merchant, in 1900 invited Bryusov to direct the art section of a projected new journal *Vega*. Nothing further developed.

FILOSOFOV, DMITRY (1872–1940). One of leading figures in "World of Art" in its early years, subsequently close to Gippius and Merezhkovsky in the religious-philosophical movement.

FOFANOV, KONSTANTIN (1862–1911). Poet, popular in 1880s, poor craftsman but possessing a genuinely musical gift.

FRICHE, VLADIMIR (1870–1929). Fellow university student of Bryusov, later a Marxist critic and historian of literature, editor.

FRIDBERG, DMITRY. Poet, contributor to *Northern Flowers*.

FYODOROV, NIKOLAI (1824–1903). Philosopher, mystic; works published posthumously. Wrote on responsibility of human beings to overcome death for sake of those who have gone before. His ideas influenced Dostoevsky, Tolstoy, Solovyov.

GAIDEBUROV, VASILY. Editor of journal *The Week,* son of Pavel Gaideburov, liberal-populist, longtime editor-publisher of the same.

GERTSYK, ADELAIDA. Essayist, poet, close friend of Marina Tsvetaeva.

GIPPIUS, VASILY. Father of Vladimir and of literary scholar Vasily.

GIPPIUS, VLADIMIR (1876–1941). Poet, literary scholar. Began poetic activity in 1895 but published little. Later director of Tenishev Gymnasium in Petersburg, where he taught Russian literature to Osip Mandelstam and Vladimir Nabokov.

GIPPIUS, ZINAIDA (sometimes HIPPIUS, 1869–1945). Leading older generation Symbolist, generally regarded as a more gifted poet than her husband, Dmitry Merezhkovsky.

GOFMAN, VIKTOR (1884–1911). Poet, follower of Balmont and Bryusov, published in Symbolist miscellanies. Later wrote prose fiction.

GOGOL, NIKOLAI (1809–1852). Author of *Dead Souls,* whose reputation as a Realist was drastically revised in writings of Bryusov, Merezhkovsky, and Bely.

GORKY, MAXIM (ALEXEI PESHKOV, 1868–1936). Most popular writer in Russia at the time of Bryusov's meeting with him. His romanticism, rather than his much acclaimed realism, was responsible for his early great success. *Foma Gordeev* was the first and best of a series of increasingly tendentious novels.

GROT, NIKOLAI (1852–1899). Philosopher, professor at Moscow University, editor of *Problems of Philosophy and Psychology*.

GUERRIER, VLADIMIR (1837–1919). Distinguished professor of ancient history at Moscow University, founder and director of a women's college (Guerrier Courses) in Moscow.

IVANOV, IVAN (1862–1929). Critic for various liberal journals in the 1890s and for *Northern Messenger,* first major journal to print Symbolist work.

IVANOV, VYACHESLAV (1866–1949). Major poet, dramatist, historian, a leading theoretician of the second generation Symbolists, who saw poetry as a *Weltanschauung*. Bryusov's friend, despite sharp polemics, for nearly two decades.

Journal for Everyone [*Žurnal dlja vsex*]. St. Petersburg, 1896–1906. Illustrated monthly with democratic orientation. Closed by government.

KAMENSKY, VLADIMIR. Schoolmate of Bryusov at Polivanov Gymnasium.

KHESIN. Decadent, member of Gryphon group, rival publishing house to Scorpion.

KHOMYAKOV, ALEXEI (1804–1860). Chief founder of the Slavophile movement, which was bent on cleansing Russia of Western influence and returning her to ancestral tradition.

KIREEVSKY, IVAN (1806–1856). Cofounder of the Slavophile movement with Khomyakov.

KLYUCHEVSKY, VASILY (1842–1911). Noted historian of Russia, professor at Moscow University and Moscow Theological Academy.

KOGAN, P. S. (1872–1932). Literary historian, critic, Marxist.

KONEVSKOY, IVAN (IVAN OREUS, 1877–1901). Philosophical and lyric poet, Konevskoy was an influential Symbolist while he lived. A posthumous volume of his work, *Poetry and Prose,* was published in 1904 by Scorpion with an introductory essay by Bryusov.

KORINFSKY, APOLLON (1868–1937). Minor poet, editor, translator.

K——OVS. KRASKOVS. Kraskov was stepfather of Elena Maslova. *See* Maslova.

KOYRANSKY, ALEXANDER, BORIS, and GENRIKH. Minor adherents to Symbolist movement in early 1900s.

KOZHEVNIKOV, V. A. Editor of the works of Nikolai Fyodorov.

KRANDIEVSKAYA, ANASTASIA. Fiction-writer, published two volumes of stories in 1905.

KURSINSKY, ALEXANDER. Minor Symbolist poet, fellow university student of Bryusov, tutor of Tolstoy's son Mikhail for some time.

LANG, ALEXANDER. Schoolmate of Bryusov, and longtime friend, minor Symbolist poet, collaborated on *Russian Symbolists*.

LEBEDEV, VLADIMIR P. Poet, prose writer.

LERMONTOV, MIKHAIL (1814–1841). Major Romantic poet, influenced by Pushkin and Byron.

LEVITAN, ISAAC (1860–1900). Important landscape painter.

Life [*Zizn'*]. St. Petersburg, 1897–1901. Literary, scientific, and political monthly. Closed by government, continued abroad.

LOKHVITSKAYA, MIRRA (1869–1905). Minor poet popular in 1890s.

LOPATIN, LEV. Idealist philosopher, psychologist, professor of Moscow University. A leader of the Moscow Psychological Society and an editor of *Problems of Philosophy and Psychology*.

LYUBOSCHÜTZ, SEMYON (1859–1926). Moscow journalist.

MASLOVA, ELENA ANDREEVNA. Early love of Bryusov who died of smallpox, May 18, 1893. *See* Introduction and Diary, note 3.

MAYAKOVSKY, VLADIMIR (1893–1930). Poet, dramatist, a leader of the Russian Futurist movement. A major literary figure of the early Soviet period, he was later attacked for individualism and "formalism." He committed suicide in 1930.

MAZURKEVICH, VLADIMIR (1871–1942). Minor poet.

MEREZHKOVSKY, DMITRY (1866–1941). Poet, novelist, critic, philosopher, married to Zinaida Gippius. In 1893 he published *On the Causes of the Present Decline and the New Currents of Contemporary Russian Literature,* which, along with his poetry collection *Symbols,* caused him to be regarded as leader of the new tendencies in the 1890s. In the early 1900s, along with Gippius, he abandoned Decadence and embarked on religious searchings.

MIKHAIL. Monk, instructor at Petersburg Theological Academy.

MIKHAILOVSKY, N. K. (1842–1904). Outstanding journalist, major exponent of populism and socialism, and important, if hostile, critic of Dostoevsky.

MINSKAYA, LYUDMILA VILKINA (VILENKINA, 1873–1920). Wife of Nikolai Minsky, herself a Decadent poetess.

MINSKY, NIKOLAI (N. M. VILENKIN, 1855–1937). Poet, editor; in 1884, in an article "An Old Quarrel," sounded the first Russian notes of Decadence. Founder of the Religious-Philosophical Society.

MINTSLOVA, ANNA. Translator of Novalis, at one time well-known in theosophist circles, in which Andrei Bely was also involved.

MIROLYUBOV, VIKTOR (1860–1939). Publisher from 1898 to 1906 of *Journal for Everyone;* friend of Chekhov.

Missionary Review [*Missionerskoe obozrenie*]. Moscow, 1896–1916. Monthly.

Monthly Essays [*Ežemesjačnye sočinenija*]. Moscow, 1900; Petersburg, 1901–1903. Monthly covering science, politics, the arts. Founded and edited by I. I. Yasinsky.

MOROZOVA, VARVARA. Wife of member of famous Moscow merchant family, patrons of the arts; subsequently wife of V. M. Sobolevsky, editor of *Russian Information,* which treated the new art kindly.

MYASOEDOV, G. G. (1835–1911). A founding member of the Wanderer group of painters. *See* Diary, note 47.

MYATLEV, IVAN (1796–1844). Poet-humorist, known for macaronic verse and for improvisations and public recitations enjoyed by Pushkin and other poets.

NADYA. *See* Bryusova, Nadezhda.

NEKRASOV, NIKOLAI (1821–1878). Major nineteenth-century poet noted for his use of folk motifs and poetic rhythms and his attention to social questions in his poetry.

NESTEROV, MIKHAIL (1862–1942). Prominent artist, independent of both the Wanderers and "World of Art."

NETTESHEIM, AGRIPPA VON (1486–1535). German scholar whose interest in magic produced legends about his life and character. He appears partially under his legendary guise in Bryusov's novel *The Fiery Angel,* but Bryusov also published and wrote material designed to illuminate his real career.

News of Foreign Literature [*Novosti inostrannoj literatury*]. Moscow, 1891–1899. Monthly literary journal with supplement of translated novels and tales.

News of the Day [*Novosti dnja*]. Moscow, 1883–1906. Daily giving coverage to literary affairs. Closed by administrative order.

New Times [*Novoe vremja*]. Petersburg, 1868–1917. Pro-government political and literary daily. Long published by Alexei Suvorin, friend and publisher of Chekhov.

New Way [*Novyj put'*]. Petersburg, 1903–1904. Continued in 1905 as *Life Questions* [*Voprosy zizni*]. Monthly first edited by Peter Pertsov and serving as organ for the Religious-Philosophical Society. Gippius and Merezhkovsky were influential contributors. *See* Diary, note 82.

NIKITIN, P. V. Philologist, academician.

Northern Messenger [*Severnyj vestnik*]. Petersburg, 1885–1898. Literary, scientific, and political journal, open to the new art from 1891.

NOUVEL, WALTER (1871–1949). Schoolfriend of Benois, member of the Pickwickians and later of "World of Art," connoisseur of music, associate of Diaghilev in his ballet enterprises.

NUROK, ALFRED (1863–1919). Member of the editorial staff of *World of Art* and specialist in French literature.

OBLEUKHOV, NIKOLAI. Editor of the journal *The Banner* and contributor to several Moscow newspapers.

OLEARIUS, ADAM (b. 1599?). German traveler and scholar; described travels in work which is one of chief sources for seventeenth-century Russian history.

ONEGIN-OTTO, ALEXANDER. Possessor of a large collection of Pushkin manuscripts eventually given to the Pushkin House, Institute of Russian Literature, Soviet Academy of Sciences.

OREUS, IVAN. *See* Konevskoy, Ivan.

PANTYUKHOV, MIKHAIL I. (1880–1910). Minor author, contemporary of Bryusov.

PAVLOVA, KAROLINA (1807–1893). Best Russian woman poet of the nineteenth century, hostess of popular Moscow literary salon. Bryusov rediscovered and acclaimed her work.

PERTSOV, PETER (1868–1947). Journalist, critic, publisher of *New Way;* belonged to Merezhkovsky's religious-philosophical circle.

PLEHVE, VYACHESLAV (1846–1904). Minister of Internal Affairs from 1902; extreme reactionary, assassinated in 1904 by Socialist Revolutionaries.

POLONSKY, YAKOV (1819–1898). Poet continuing the romantic tradition into the later nineteenth century.

POLYAKOV, SERGEI (1874–1948). Maecenas to Moscow Symbolists, from enlightened merchant background. Founder of publishing house Scorpion, mathematician, translator, accomplished linguist.

POSSE, VLADIMIR. Editor of journal *Life,* organ of legal Marxism.

Problems of Philosophy and Psychology [*Voprosy filosofii i psixologii*]. Moscow, 1890–1918. Four or five times a year. Scholarly journal, organ of the Moscow Psychological Society.

PUSHKIN, ALEXANDER (1799–1837). Founder of modern Russian poetry.

RACHINSKY, GREGORY (1859–1939). Translator, editor, close to the Symbolists, especially Bely. Editor of works of Vladimir Solovyov and Nietzsche.

RAZIN, STENKA (STEPAN). Cossack leader of bloody peasant rebellion in 1670–1671, commemorated in song and story.

Rebus [*Rebus*]. Petersburg, 1882–1916. Weekly journal of spiritualism and psychic exploration.

REDON, ODILON (1840–1916). French painter, engraver, whose work exemplified Decadent and Symbolist moods. Reproductions of his works appeared in *The Balance*.

REMIZOV, ALEXEI (1877–1957). Important prose writer with ties to Gogol, Dostoevsky, and Leskov; he exercised a powerful influence on the twentieth-century school of "ornamental prose."

REPIN, ILYA (1844–1930). Leading member of the Wanderer group (*See* Diary, note 47), noted for portraits and historical paintings.

Review of the Picturesque [*Živopisnoe obozrenie*]. Petersburg, 1872–1902, 1904–1905. Weekly illustrated journal of travel and discovery. Monthly literary and political supplement published 1882–1894, 1902.

ROSLAVLEV, ALEXANDER (1883–1920). Poet, early follower of Bryusov and Balmont, later wrote naturalistic fiction.

ROZANOV, VASILY (1856–1919). Writer, philosopher, noted for his mystical treatment of sexuality. His book, *Dostoevsky's "Legend of the Grand Inquisitor"* (1894), is an important statement on Russian nihilism.

Russian Archive [*Russkij arxiv*]. Moscow, 1863–1917. Historical and literary monthly, long published by Peter Bartenev.

Russian Bulletin [*Russkij listok*]. Moscow, 1890–1906. Daily paper without pre-publication censorship.

Russian Information [*Russkie vedomosti*]. Moscow, 1863–1918. Daily paper, grew in literary importance in the 1880s. Somewhat encouraging in the '90s toward the new art.

Russian Review [*Russkoe obozrenie*]. Moscow, 1890–1898 (sporadically in 1901 and 1903). Literary, political, and scientific monthly, conservative and nationalist in tone, printing a wide range of writers, including Symbolists.

Russian Thought [*Russkaja mysl'*]. Moscow, 1880–1912; Moscow and Petersburg, 1912–1918. Liberal literary, social, and political monthly. In 1908 Peter Struve joined the journal and was its leading figure from 1910 on. Philosophers Berdyaev, Bulgakov, and others published there during its later period. Bryusov was its literary editor from 1910 to 1912.

SABASHNIKOV, MIKHAIL (1871–1943). With his brother Sergei (1873–1909), founded a Moscow publishing house in 1891 primarily for cultural ends. They published many outstanding works and series.

SABLIN, VLADIMIR (1872–1916). Publisher, translator of Maeterlinck, Ibsen and others.

SAFONOV, SERGEI (1867–1904). Poet and prose writer.

SAMYGIN, MIKHAIL (pseudonym MARK KRINITSKY, 1874–1952). Minor fiction writer, at first Symbolist in manner, later turning to Realism.

SATIN, ALEXANDER. Schoolmate of Bryusov at Polivanov Gymnasium in Moscow.

SAVITSKAYA, LUDMILA (LUCY). Translator of Maeterlinck.

SAVODNIK, VLADIMIR (1874–1940). Minor Symbolist poet, author of two-volume history of Russian literature used as standard textbook till the end of the 1920s.

SCHICK, MAXIMILIAN (1884–1968). Poet and translator, wrote in both Russian and German. Early follower of Bryusov and Balmont, member of staff of *The Balance*.

SEMYONOV, MIKHAIL. Active in planning and managing *The Balance;* his views were often at odds with Bryusov's.

SH. Presumably SHESTERKINA, ANNA. *See* Shesterkina.

SHABLIOVSKY. Classmate of Bryusov at Moscow University.

SHAGINIAN, MARIETTA (b. 1888). Poet, journalist,

novelist, critic, began publication in 1903, still active in 1970s.

SHALYAPIN (CHALIAPIN), FYODOR (1873–1938). Russian basso.

SHARAPOV, SERGEI (1855–1911). Conservative writer on agricultural questions.

SHEFFER, VALERIAN (1864–1900). Professor of classical philology at Moscow University.

SHESTERKIN, MIKHAIL (1866–1908). Moscow artist, art critic for *The Balance*, painted subjects from Bryusov's and Balmont's poems.

SHESTERKINA, ANNA. Wife of artist Mikhail, and recipient of over two hundred letters from Bryusov. Their relationship was closest in 1900–1902.

SHESTOV, LEV (LEV SHVARTSMAN, 1866–1938). Philosopher and literary critic, influenced by Nietzsche and Kierkegaard. Wrote on links between Dostoevsky and Nietzsche, Tolstoy and Nietzsche.

SHULYATIKOV, VLADIMIR (1872–1912). Marxist literary critic, Bolshevik, whose name was later given to the deviationist trend called vulgar sociologism.

SKIRMUNT, S. Publisher.

SKITALETS ("Wanderer"; STEPAN PETROV, 1869–1941). Follower of Gorky, often wrote on subjects dealing with lower classes.

SKVORTSOV, VASILY. Editor-publisher of *Missionary Survey*.

SLUCHEVSKY, KONSTANTIN (1837–1904). Talented poet who became the object of a hostile press campaign by the radical critics of the sixties and forced into exile. Resumed publication in the 1880s.

SOBOLEVSKY, SERGEI. Philologist, professor of Greek at Moscow University.

SOKOLOV, SERGEI (pseudonym SERGEI KRECHETOV, 1878–1936). Founder in 1903 of publishing house Gryphon, rival and imitator of Scorpion. Husband of Nina Petrovskaya. *See* the Introduction.

SOLOGUB, FYODOR (FYODOR TETERNIKOV, 1863–1927). Major representative of older generation of Symbolists. His short stories and poems appearing from the 1880s earned him tag of Decadent. His best-known novel, *The Petty Demon* (1907), links him to Gogol and Dostoevsky.

SOLOVYOV, MIKHAIL (1862–1903). Brother of Vladimir, editor of his works.

SOLOVYOV, VLADIMIR (1853–1900). Philosopher, poet, mystic, liberal polemicist; brilliant, cultured, a follower of Fet in his poetry and an important influence on the development of Russian Symbolism.

Southern Review [*Južnoe obozrenie*]. Odessa, 1896–1906 (*Odessa Gazette* [*Odesskaja gazeta*], 1907–1909). Daily paper covering wide range of topics, including literature. Liberal slant.

STANYUKOVICH, VLADIMIR (1873–1939). Bryusov's closest friend in the Kreyman Gymnasium, where he introduced Bryusov to Russian literature.

STAVROGIN, NIKOLAI. Protagonist of Dostoevsky's novel *The Possessed*.

SUMAROKOV, ALEXANDER (1718–1777). A leading poet and dramatist of Russian Classicism.

TOLSTOY, COUNT ALEXEI K. (1817–1875). Poet, novelist, author of important trilogy of historical dramas.

TOLSTOY, COUNT LEO (1828–1910). The author of *War and Peace* and *Anna Karenina,* was particularly unreceptive to the new art. *See* Diary, note 25.

TRUBETSKAYA, PRINCESS. One of a rather numerous princely Moscow family.

TURGENEV, IVAN (1818–1883). Author of *Fathers and Sons* and other major novels. He had admirers among the Symbolists, such as Alexander Blok, but Bryusov was not among them.

Turning Point, The [*Pereval*]. Moscow, 1906–1907. (Subtitle: *Journal of Free Thought*.) Monthly journal of literary and social comment. Editor: S. A. Sokolov.

Universal Illustration [*Vsemirnaja illjustracija*]. Petersburg, 1869–1917?. Weekly illustrated magazine.

VASNETSOV, VIKTOR (1848–1926). Member of Moscow circle of artists based at Abramtsevo, estate of Savva Mamontov, having special interest in medieval Russian art and folklore. Joined "World of Art."

VEYNBERG (WEINBERG), PETER (pseudonym HEINE FROM TAMBOV [PODUNK], 1831–1908). Poet and translator.

VIKTOROV, DAVID. Philosopher, instructor at Moscow University.

VINOGRADOV, PAVEL (SIR PAUL VINOGRADOFF, 1854–1925). Historian, professor at Moscow then at Cambridge University from 1903. Knighted in 1917.

VOLOSHIN, MAXIMILIAN (1877–1932). Poet and artist, world-traveler whose travels are widely reflected in his poetry. Translator of French poets.

VOLYNSKY, A. (AKIM FLEKSER, 1863–1926). Early ideologist of Symbolists, *de facto* editor of *Northern Messenger* till journal's close in 1898.

VRUBEL, MIKHAIL (1856–1910). Major Russian artist whose work, which strove to develop a new artistic vocabulary, was highly sympathetic to the Symbolist mood.

VYAZEMSKY, PRINCE PETER (1792–1878). Intimate of Pushkin, and a leading Romantic poet.

World of Art [*Mir iskusstva*]. Petersburg, 1899–1904. Illustrated art monthly which for a time combined the new trends in both art and literature. Among its active participants were Bryusov, Gippius, Merezhkovsky, Diaghilev, Benois, and other prominent figures. *See* also Diary, note 86.

YAKOVLEV. Schoolmate of Bryusov at Polivanov Gymnasium.

YASHCHENKO, ALEXANDER. Jurist; university acquaintance of Bryusov.

YASINSKY, IERONYM (pseudonym MAXIM BELINSKY, 1850–1931). Writer, one of first to articulate Symbolist ideas (1884); journalist; editor of *Monthly Essays,* 1900–1903.

YASUNINSKY, MIKHAIL. Schoolmate of Bryusov at Polivanov Gymnasium in Moscow.

YUZHIN-SUMBATOV, ALEXANDER (PRINCE ALEXANDER SUMBATOV, 1857–1927). Actor, dramatist, theater director. Associated with Maly Theatre in Moscow from 1882 and one of the founders of the Moscow Literary-Artistic Circle. *See* the Introduction.

ZHDANOV, LEV (LEV GELMAN). Poet, dramatist, author of historical novels.

ZHUKOVSKY, VASILY (1783–1852). Romantic poet, predecessor of Pushkin, translator of German and English poetry of Sentimental and Romantic periods.

Selected Bibliography

Bryusov. Collected Works.

Bryusov's works of poetry, fiction, and criticism are not listed separately in this bibliography but may be found in the 1976 Russian bibliography published in Erevan, Soviet Armenia. His novel *Fiery Angel* and some of his shorter fiction such as "Republic of the Southern Cross" have long been available in English translation. Of his poems only a handful are to be found anthologized in translation. Two multi-volume Russian collected editions have been attempted, one in his lifetime and one for the centenary of his birth:

Brjusov, Valerij. *Polnoe sobranie sočinenij i perevodov* [*Complete Collected Works and Translations*]. Vols. 1, 2, 3, 4, 12, 13, 15, 21. Petersburg: Sirin, 1913–1914.

    The projected number of volumes was twenty-five.

———. *Sobranie sočinenij v semi tomax* [*Collected Works in Seven Volumes*]. N. S. Ašukin, et al., eds. Moscow: Xudožestvennaja literatura, 1973–1975.

    This edition, while useful and well edited, does not pretend to completeness. Among other omissions, Bryusov's short fiction is entirely absent.

Critical and Biographical Works on Bryusov

A. English and German

Binyon, T. J. "Bibliography of the Works of Valery Bryusov." *Oxford Slavonic Papers* 12 (1965): 117–140.

    Until the 1976 Soviet publication (q.v.), the fullest Bryusov bibliography. (Mistakenly listed in Rice's book as a 1956 publication.)

———. "Valery Bryusov and the Nature of Art." *Oxford Slavonic Papers* 7 (1974): 96–111.

> Traces the development of some aspects of Bryusov's critical views on art throughout his career.

Donchin, Georgette. *The Influence of French Symbolism on Russian Poetry.* The Hague: Mouton, 1958.

> With chapters on "The Symbolist Press," "The Symbolist Aesthetics," "Themes in Symbolist Poetry," and "The Symbolist Technique," along with an extensive bibliography, this work is a source on the Russian Symbolist movement itself, as well as its French links.

Erlich, Victor. "The Maker and the Seer: Two Russian Symbolists." In *The Double Image: Concepts of the Poet in Slavic Literatures.* Baltimore: Johns Hopkins, 1964.

> Comparison and contrast of careers, themes and poetic methods of Bryusov and Alexander Blok.

Holthusen, Johannes. *Studien zur Ästhetik und Poetik des Russischen Symbolismus.* Gottingen: Vandenhoeck and Ruprecht, 1957.

> Includes chapters comparing the lyrics of Bryusov and Alexander Blok during the early period of both writers' work, with close analysis of texts for technique and theme.

Maslenikov, Oleg A. *The Frenzied Poets: Andrei Biely and the Russian Symbolists.* Berkeley and Los Angeles: University of California Press, 1952.

> Bely's career and his relations with prominent Symbolists, among them Bryusov. Bibliography.

Poggioli, Renato. *Poets of Russia, 1890–1930.* Cambridge, Mass.: Harvard University Press, 1960.

> A survey of movements in modern Russian poetry: Decadence, Symbolism, Acmeism, Futurism, and after. Five of ten chapters deal with the first two topics and with poets who fall into those groups. Bibliography.

Rice, Martin P. *Briusov and the Rise of Russian Symbolism.* Ann Arbor: Ardis, 1975.

> This brief volume summarizes Bryusov's career on the basis of material long available in Russian but only in scattered fashion in English.

Schmidt, Alexander. *Valerij Brjusovs Beitrag zur Literaturtheorie. Aus der Geschichte des Russischen Symbolismus.* Slavistische Beiträge, vol. 7. Munich: Otto Sagner, 1963.

> Analysis of Bryusov's views of the poet and poetry with declared emphasis on his Russian sources. Bibliography.

Setschkareff (Setchkarev), V. "The Narrative Prose of Brjusov." *International Journal of Linguistics and Poetics* 1/2 (1959): 237–265.

> Only extensive treatment in English of Bryusov's prose fiction by a specialist in Russian Symbolism.

Struk, Danylo. "The Great Escape: Principal Themes in Valerij Brjusov's Poetry." *Slavic and East European Journal* 12 (1968): 407–423.

> Interpretation of Bryusov's poetry as aesthetic escapism along three lines: "loneliness, love, and lore" (history, myth, prophecy).

West, James. *Russian Symbolism: A Study of Vyacheslav Ivanov and the Russian Symbolist Aesthetic.* London: Methuen, 1970.

> Along with Ivanov's theories, includes a lengthy section on the "Symbolist Debate" on the relation of art to reality. Bibliography.

B. Russian

Ajvazjan, K. V., et al., eds. *Brjusovskie čtenija 1962* [*Readings on Bryusov*]. Erevan: Armjanskoe gosudarstvennoe izdatel'stvo, 1963.

———. *Brjusovskie čtenija 1963*. Erevan: Izdatel'stvo 'Ajastan', 1964.

———. *Brjusovskie čtenija 1966*. Erevan: Izdatel'stvo 'Ajastan', 1968.

———. *Brjusovskie čtenija 1971*. Erevan: Izdatel'stvo 'Ajastan', 1973.

———. *Brjusovskie čtenija 1973*. Erevan: Izdatel'stvo 'Sovetakan grox', 1976.

> Collections of articles, reminiscences, and informational notes on Bryusov, with some emphasis on his interest in and work as translator of Armenian poetry.

Asmus, V., et al. *Literaturnoe nasledstvo* [*Literary Heritage*]. Vol 27–28. Moscow: Žurnal'no-gazetnoe ob"edinenie, 1937.

> An early publication in this series, begun in 1931. Collection of documentary materials pertaining to Russian Symbolism.

Ašukin, N., ed. *Valerij Brjusov v avtobiografičeskix zapisjax, pis'max, vospominanijax sovremennikov i otzyvov kritiki* [*Valery Bryusov in Autobiographical Notes, Letters, Recollections of Contemporaries and Critical Notices*]. Moscow: Federacija, 1929.

> Year-by-year chronicle of Bryusov's life and career.

Maksimov, D. *Poezija Valerija Brjusova*. Leningrad: Xudožestvennaja literatura, 1940.

> Literary and biographical study of Bryusov with emphasis on his poetry. First book-length treatment since the twenties. Informative though one-sided.

———. *Brjusov. Poezija i pozicija* [*Poetry and Position*]. Leningrad: Sovetskij pisatel', 1969.

> Maksimov's second study puts strong stress on Bryusov's development in the 1890s and on his position in regard to the revolutions of 1905 and 1917.

Močul'skij, Konstantin. *Valerij Brjusov*. Paris: YMCA Press, 1962.

> An émigré scholar's treatment of Bryusov, limited by lack of archival material but aided by absence of censorship. No bibliography or footnotes.

Muratova, K. D., ed. *Bibliografija V. Ja. Brjusova, 1884–1973*. Erevan: Erevan University Press, 1976.

> For all purposes the definitive bibliography of Bryusov works (1,850 items, up to 1974) and a very full and detailed listing of works about him (2,476 items).

Ščerbina, V. R., et al., eds. *Literaturnoe nasledstvo*. Vol. 85. Moscow: "Nauka," 1976.

> Entire volume devoted to Bryusov—reminiscences, letters, unpublished poetry, prose and criticism, surveys of aspects of his work.

Selected Memoir Literature in Russian

A. By Valery Bryusov

Dnevniki [*Diaries*]. Moscow: M. and S. Sabašnikov, 1927. Letchworth: Bradda, 1972.

Iz moej žizni. Moja junost'. Pamjati. [*From My Life. My Youth. Recollections*]. Moscow: M. and S. Sabašnikov, 1927.

> Introduction to an unwritten autobiographical poem. Fictionalized autobiography written in 1900. Fragment of reminiscences.

B. About Valery Bryusov

Belyj, Andrej. *Načalo veka* [*The Beginning of the Century*]. Moscow-Leningrad: Gosudarstvennoe izdatel'stvo xudožestvennoj literatury, 1933. Reprint, Chicago: Russian Language Specialties, 1966.

Brjusova, Ioanna. "Materialy k biografii Valerija Brjusova." In V. Brjusov, *Izbrannye stixi* [Selected Poems], pp. 119–149. Moscow: Academia, 1933.

> Concise biographical sketch by Bryusov's wife including some material not found elsewhere. An unpublished memoir by Joanna Bryusov has been referred to in some Soviet sources.

Čulkov, Georgij. "Brjusov." In *Gody stranstvij* [*Years of Wandering*], pp. 89–107. Moscow: Federacija, 1930.

Cvetaeva [Tsvetaeva], Marina. "Geroj truda (zapisi o Valerii Brjusove)" ["Hero of Labor (Notes about Valery Bryusov)"]. In *Proza* [*Prose*], pp. 203–270. New York: Chekhov Publishing House, 1953.

> First printed in *Volja Rossii* 9–10 (1925): 42–68; 11 (1925).

Gippius, Zinaida, "Oderžimyj (O Brjusove)" ["The Possessed One (About Bryusov)"]. In *Živye lica* [*Living Personages*], pp. 73–117. Prague: Plamja, 1925.

Petrovskaja, Nina. "Iz 'Vospominanij'" ["From 'Recollections'"]. *Literaturnoe nasledstvo* 85 (1976): 773–798.

Xodasevič [Khodasevich], V. F. "Brjusov." In *Nekropol'* [*Necropolis*], pp. 26–60. Brussels: Les Editions Petropolis, 1939; Paris: YMCA Press, 1976.

Index

About Art, 68, 69, 74, 75, 79, 85, 91
Akhmatova, Anna, 3
Aksakov, Konstantin, 72, 81
Allegro, 84
Amozov, Lev, 95
Andreevsky, Sergei, 108, 114
Andreyev, Leonid, 114, 116, 129, 130, 131, 137
Antonin, Bishop, 132
Aristophanes, 43
Armenia, poetry collection edited by Bryusov, 13–14
Art, 153
Artist, 35
Athenaeum, 114

Bachmann, Georg, 78, 79, 91, 101, 127
Bakst, Leon, 124, 133
Balance, The, 2, 6, 11, 12, 13, 15, 18, 27, 99n, 137, 153
Balmont, Ekaterina, 126, 127
Balmont, Konstantin, 14, 16, 25–26, 40, 41, 42, 44, 45, 49, 53, 54, 55, 56, 61, 70, 72, 73, 74, 75, 76, 77, 78, 79–80, 81, 82, 83, 85–86, 87, 91–92, 95, 100, 101, 107, 108, 109, 110, 111, 112, 114, 126, 127, 136, 137, 138, 152, 161, 162n
Baltrushaitis, Yurgis, 91, 92, 93, 94, 96–97, 99n, 100, 101, 103, 104, 105, 106, 109, 117, 120, 121, 127, 130
Banner, The, 78
Baratynsky, Evgeny, 5, 23, 72, 92
Bartenev, Peter, 71–72, 81, 99, 100–101, 110
Bartenev, Yury, 72, 96, 100, 101, 102, 117, 123, 127
Bashkirtseva, Marie, 30
Batyushkov, Konstantin, 100

Baudelaire, Charles, 1, 5, 8, 11, 17, 26, 163
Bazhenov, Nikolai, 14, 130, 144
Beardsley, Aubrey, 6
Bely, Andrei, 2, 3, 4, 14, 16, 17, 18, 19, 27, 30, 115, 119, 121, 122, 130, 137, 140, 142, 151, 152, 154
Benedikt, 132
Benois, Alexander, 123, 124, 135
Berdyaev, Nikolai, 14, 131
Bible, 10, 48, 51, 52
Bilibin, Ivan, 94
Blok, Alexander, 2, 3, 4, 5, 130, 152
Blok, Lyubov Dmitrievna, 17
Boborykin, Peter, 81, 103, 123, 129
Bobrov, Sergei, 172
Boileau, Nicholas, 52
Book of Meditations, A, 80, 93
Borodaevsky, Valerian, 129
Bryusov, Alexander, 9, 59, 145
Bryusova, Eugenia, 158
Bryusova, Joanna Runt, 22, 23, 24, 35, 53, 57n, 59, 61, 67, 70, 71, 79, 81, 90, 109, 120, 136, 140n, 158
Bryusova, Nadezhda, 25, 46n, 57, 67, 69, 70, 79, 140n, 155
Budantsev, Sergei, 171, 172
Bugaev. *See* Bely, Andrei
Bugaev, Nikolai, 121n, 140
Bulgakov, Alexander, 100
Bulgakov, Sergei, 131
Bunin, Ivan, 75, 78, 80–81, 82, 91, 95, 101, 102, 115, 130
Burenin, Viktor, 92
Byron, George Gordon, Lord, 7

Calderón de la Barca, Pedro, 74, 80
Chefs d'oeuvre, 8–9, 31, 42, 43, 44, 45, 46, 56n, 72, 73, 107, 150

Chekhov, Anton, 2, 105, 111, 115–116, 122, 130n, 141n
Chernigovets (-Vishnevsky), Fyodor, 132
Chernogubov, Nikolai, 96, 113, 114
Chirikov, Evgeny, 105, 106
Chirikova, Mme., 105
Chulkov, Georgy, 109, 110, 114, 123, 129
Chyumina, Olga, 84
Commissariat of Education, 15, 170–171
Communism, 32, 159
Corneille, Pierre, 115

D'Annunzio, Gabriel, 109
Decadence, 2, 3, 7, 9, 10, 17, 22, 23, 25, 26, 36, 37, 40n, 42, 43, 44, 76, 95, 103, 115, 118, 119, 120, 133, 137, 138, 139, 149, 150, 164n
Dedlov, V., 133
Dehmel, Richard, 124
Delvig, Baron, 11
Derzhavin, G. R., 100
Descartes, René, 70
Diaghilev, Sergei, 92, 111, 133, 134
Dobrolyubov, Alexander, 25, 26, 39, 40, 43, 46, 50, 51, 61, 62–69, 70–71, 72, 73, 74, 78, 79, 82, 97–99, 120, 124, 134–135, 136, 140–141, 142, 143n, 155
Dolgorukov, Princes Peter and Paul, 144
Dosekin, N. V., 96
Dostoevsky, Fyodor, 4, 5, 6, 46, 47, 94n, 102, 107, 132, 140
Dukhobors, 134n, 141
Dumas, Alexandre, 42
Durnov, Modest, 78, 80, 103, 109, 120

Earth's Axis, The, 99n, 123n
Eda. *See* Bryusova, Joanna Runt
Egorov, Efim, 140

Ehrenburg, Ilya, 21–22
Eliot, T. S., 1
Ellis, 165n, 166n
Erlich, Yakov, 82n, 120
Ermilov, Vladimir, 104
Experiments, 169

Feigin, Yakov, 123
Fet, Afanasy, 5, 49, 96, 112, 113, 115, 122
Fiedler, Friedrich, 76–77
Fiery Angel, The, 18, 19, 20, 143, 156, 161, 162, 164, 172
Filosofov, Dmitry, 125n, 128n, 133, 134, 136
Flekser, Akim. *See* Volynsky-Flekser, Akim
Fofanov, Konstantin, 83, 84
Frenkel, 123
Friche, Vladimir, 43
Fridberg, Dmitry, 110
Futurism, 6
Fyodorov, Nikolai, 31, 96

Gaideburov, Vasily, 76
Gautier, Théophile, 1
Gertsyk, Adelaida, 162
Ghil, René, 6
Gippius, Vasily, 124
Gippius, Vladimir, 25, 39, 40, 46, 63, 64, 65, 78, 87
Gippius, Zinaida, 7, 19, 20, 21, 23, 27, 28, 29, 30, 74, 75, 77, 80, 81–82, 108, 109, 110, 112, 114, 117–118, 119, 120, 121, 122, 123, 125, 128, 130n, 131, 133, 134, 135, 140, 154
Gofman, Viktor, 137
Gogol, Nikolai, 47
Goldstein, Mme., 139
Gorky, Maxim, 2, 13, 14, 102, 104–107, 110, 111n, 112, 130, 131, 136, 149n
Gourmont, Remy de, 6
Goya, Francisco, 74
Grot, Nikolai, 41
Gryphon publishing house, 137, 153

Guerrier, Vladimir, 51, 57, 86, 87, 88

Hamsun, Knut, 11
Homer, 4, 10, 36, 48
How to End the War?, 159

Ibsen, Henrik, 11, 85
Impressionism, 96
Ivanov, Ivan, 40, 109
Ivanov, Vyacheslav, 3, 139
Izvekov, 89

Kamensky, Vladimir, 37
Kant, Immanuel, 52, 53, 107, 141n
Khesin, 137
Khodasevich, Vladislav, 14–15, 18, 19, 20, 21, 22, 24, 28, 30, 170, 171
Khomyakov, Alexei, 81
Kireevsky, Ivan, 72
Klyuchevsky, Vasily, 51, 57, 87
Kogan, P. S., 104
Konevskoy, Ivan. *See* Oreus, Ivan
Korinfsky, Apollon, 44, 77, 78, 85
K——ovs (Kraskovs), 35, 36
Koyransky(s), Alexander, Boris, Genrikh, 129, 137
Kozakov (folk satirist), 63
Kozhevnikov, V. A., 96
Krandievskaya, Anastasia, 123
Krechetov-Sokolov, Sergei, 17, 137
Kurskinsky, Alexander, 42, 43, 44, 45, 72, 74, 78, 109, 121, 123, 127

Laforgue, Jules, 22
Lang, Alexander, 24–25, 37, 38, 39, 40, 43, 78, 79, 89, 94, 100, 101
Lebedev, Vladimir, 78
Leibniz, Gottfried Wilhelm von, 53
Lentovsky, Mikhail, 110
Lermontov, Mikhail, 16, 83
Levitan, Isaac, 96
Life, 111
Lokhvitskaya, Mirra, 55, 84, 85

Lvova, Nadezhda, 20, 21, 22
Lyuboschütz, Semyon, 129, 139

Maeterlinck, Maurice, 6, 8, 45, 52, 53, 82
Mallarmé, Stéphane, 2, 5, 8, 36, 80
Maly Theater, 14
Mandelstam, Osip, 3
Marlowe, Christopher, 83, 85
Maslova, Elena Andreevna, 16, 17, 21, 36, 37, 51
Mayakovsky, Vladimir, 3, 6
Mazurkevich, Vladimir, 76, 77
Me eum esse, 9–10, 31, 45, 46, 48, 49, 55, 72, 73
Merezhkovsky, Dmitry, 27, 28, 37, 74–75, 77, 81, 82, 83, 84, 85, 92, 102, 108, 109, 112, 116, 117, 118, 119, 120, 121, 122, 124, 125, 126, 131, 132, 133, 134, 135, 136–137, 140
Messenger of Europe, 7
Mikhail (monk), 132
Mikhailovsky, N. K., 116
Minskaya, Lyudmila Vilkina, 107, 108, 133, 140n
Minsky, Nikolai, 75, 78, 82, 107, 108, 111, 132, 133, 136
Mintslova, Anna, 121
Mirolyubov, Viktor, 132
Modernism, 151, 152
Molokans, 134
Monthly Essays, 110n, 111
Morozova, Varvara, 103, 109, 110
Moscow Art Theatre, 104, 122, 130n, 136n, 138
Moscow Literary-Artistic Circle, 14, 15, 122, 123, 128, 129, 130, 136–138, 139, 155
Moscow Psychological Society, 121
Mozart, Wolfgang Amadeus, 154
Musset, Alfred de, 23
Myasoedov, G. G., 96
Myatlev, Ivan, 132
My Youth, 16, 29, 30, 99n

Nadson, Semyon, 7
Nadya. *See* Bryusova, Nadezhda

Nekrasov, Nikolai, 4, 136
Nemirovich-Danchenko, Vladimir, 104n
Nesterov, Mikhail, 96
Nettesheim, Agrippa von, 103
News of Foreign Literature, 35, 36
News of the Day, 40, 41, 43, 44, 149
New Times, 38, 105, 107
New Way, 27, 125n, 128, 131, 133, 135, 140, 162n
Nietzsche, Friedrich, 74–75, 96
Nikitin, P. V., 88
Nilender, Vladimir, 166n
Northern Flowers, 11, 12, 102, 108–109, 110–111, 115, 116n, 127, 133
Northern Messenger, 30, 45
Notes of the Fatherland, 95
Nouvel, Walter, 124, 133
Novalis, 52
Nurok, Alfred, 124

Obleukhov, Nikolai, 78, 80
Olearius, Adam, 57
Olovyanishnikova, M. I., 93
Onegin-Otto, Alexander, 139
Oreus, Ivan, 26, 78, 80, 81, 94, 97, 110, 114, 120, 128, 154
Ovid, 37

Pantyukhov, Mikhail I., 129
Parnassian movement, 1
Pasternak, Boris, 3
Pavlova, Karolina, 82
Pertsov, Peter, 92, 95, 110, 111, 128, 131, 133, 135, 140, 162n
Petrovskaya, Nina, 12, 17, 18, 19, 20, 21, 24, 26, 114n, 143n, 149n, 156, 157, 158
Petrovsky, Aleksei, 119, 121
Pilsky, 31
Plaksin, 121
Plehve, Vyacheslav, 128
Plutarch, 42
Poe, Edgar Allan, 4, 6, 8, 10, 26, 44, 45, 53, 107
Poems to/by Nelli, 21
Poggioli, Renato, 5

Polonsky, Yakov, 75
Polyakov, Sergei, 11, 91, 92, 93, 94, 100, 101, 102, 103, 107, 108, 110, 111, 112, 116, 117, 119, 120, 127, 140
Posse, Vladimir, 104, 105, 106
Prévost, Marcel, 164, 165
Problems of Philosophy and Psychology, 56n, 85
Pushkin, Alexander, 3, 4, 5, 6, 11, 36, 38, 52, 59, 72, 84, 100, 107, 132, 139

Rachinsky, Gregory, 142
Racine, Jean, 115
Realism, 1
Rebus, 35, 151
Redon, Odilon, 6, 139
Régnier, Henri de, 78
Religious-Philosophical Society, 125, 128n, 131–132
Remizov, Alexei, 129, 130–131
Repin, Ilya, 96
Review of the Picturesque, 36
Revolution of 1905, 12, 143n, 144–145
Revolution of 1917, 15, 28, 149n, 159, 170
Rilke, Rainer Maria von, 124
Rimbaud, Arthur, 2, 52
Romanticism, 10, 16, 23, 52, 82, 164
Rosenberg, Klara, 129
Roslavlev, Alexander, 137
Rostand, Edmond, 163, 164, 165
Rousseau, Jean-Jacques, 29, 51, 87
Rozanov, Vasily, 55, 108n, 110, 111, 119, 124, 132
Ruskin, John, 102
Russian Archive, 6, 11, 71, 73, 101, 110, 110n
Russian Bulletin, 44, 103, 122, 125n, 127n
Russian Review, 36, 37
Russian Symbolists, 8, 24–25, 38, 39, 40, 56
Russian Thought, 13, 167n, 169n

Sabashnikov, Mikhail, 112
Sablin, Vladimir, 130
Sadovskoy, Boris, 155
Safonov, Sergei, 76, 77
Salieri, Antonio, 154
Samygin, Mikhail, 44, 61, 62, 68
Sand, George, 23
Satin, Alexander, 37
Savitskaya, Lucy, 126
Savodnik, Vladimir, 78, 86, 104, 121
Schick, Maximilian, 137, 138
Scorpion publishing house, 11, 12, 27, 101, 102, 103, 107, 111, 112, 114n, 115, 116, 117, 121, 123n, 135, 137, 144, 153
Semyonov, Mikhail, 133
Sh., 93, 102, 103, 110, 140n. *See also* Shesterkina, Anna
Shabliovsky, 88
Shaginian, Marietta, 167
Shakespeare, William, 10, 48, 78, 79, 107
Shalyapin, Fyodor, 130
Sheffer, Valerian, 88
Shelley, Percy Bysshe, 72, 107
Shesterkin, Mikhail, 96, 102, 103
Shesterkina, Anna, 93n, 99n, 102, 140n
Shestov, Lev, 136
Shulyatikov, Vladimir, 44
Sirin publishing house, 13, 149
Skirmunt, S., 104
Skitalets ("Wanderer"), 130
Skvortsov, Vasily, 132
Sluchevsky, Konstantin, 75, 76, 77, 82, 83, 85, 125, 132
Sobolevsky, Sergei, 88
Socialist Realism, 32
Society of Amateurs of Western Literature, 40, 137
Sokolov, Sergei. *See* Krechetov-Sokolov, Sergei
Sologub, Fyodor, 50, 75, 76, 77, 78, 80, 96, 125, 132, 152
Solovyov, Mikhail, 102, 103, 115, 118, 119
Solovyov, Sergei, 115, 151–152

Solovyov, Vladimir, 8, 96, 100, 101, 102, 104, 115
Solovyova, Olga Mikhailovna, 102, 103, 115, 118, 119, 125–126
Somov, Konstantin, 124
Southern Review, 80, 81
Spinoza, Benedict, 37
Stanislavsky, Konstantin, 104n
Stanyukovich, Vladimir, 109
Stephanos, 12, 18, 143, 144, 152, 154n
Strindberg, August, 93
Struve, Peter, 13
Sumarokov, Alexander, 52
Sumbatov-Yuzhin, Prince Andrei, 14, 129
Suvorin, Aleksei, 107
Symbolism, 1, 2, 3, 4, 7, 9, 11, 12, 13, 15, 16, 17, 24, 25, 26, 28, 36, 37, 39, 40, 45, 48, 51, 64, 102, 104, 121n, 133, 157, 165

Tacitus, 115
Tertia Vigilia, 10–11, 24, 29, 30, 53, 60, 100, 101, 103, 107, 108, 110n, 150
Those Far and Near, 137n, 168
Tolstaya, Countess Sophia, 113
Tolstoy, Count Alexei Konstantinovich, 76
Tolstoy, Count Leo, 2, 6, 42, 43, 47, 56, 68n, 75, 95, 96, 107, 111n, 112, 113, 114, 130, 139n, 141, 142n, 143n
Trankvilitsky, 88
Trubetskaya, Princess, 121
Tsar Maximilian, 94
Tsvetaeva, Marina, 3, 30, 31, 153
Turgenev, Ivan, 46, 47
Turning-Point, The, 153
Tyutchev, Fyodor, 5, 26, 71, 72, 79, 81, 100, 172

Universal Illustration, 39
Urbi et orbi, 4, 11, 12, 18, 31, 99n, 162, 163
Urusov, Prince Andrei, 14

Vasnetsov, Viktor, 105
Vergil, 51, 99, 115
Verhaeren, Emile, 2, 6, 78, 93, 103, 124, 129–130
Verlaine, Paul, 2, 6, 8, 17, 35, 37, 44, 57, 124, 143
Viele-Griffin, Francis, 78, 124
Viktorov, David, 123
Vinogradov, Pavel, 57, 88
Voloshin, Maximilian, 136, 137, 154, 162, 167
Volynsky-Flekser, Akim, 116, 121, 126
Vrubel, Mikhail, 77
Vyazemsky, Prince Peter, 81

Wanderers, The, 96, 133n
Weinberg, Peter, 82–83

Wilde, Oscar, 102, 103
World of Art, 92n, 111, 114, 115, 118–119, 121, 130n, 133, 134, 135, 137n

Yakovlev, 37
Yashchenko, Alexander, 110, 123, 129, 130, 139
Yasinsky, Ieronym, 110
Yasyuninsky, Mikhail, 37
Yuzhin. *See* Sumbatov-Yuzhin, Prince Andrei

Zaitsev, Boris, 14
Zhdanov, Lev, 103
Zhukovsky, Vasily, 100
Zola, Emile, 57

Designer:	Wolfgang Lederer
Compositor:	Interactive Composition Corp.
Printer:	Thomson-Shore, Inc.
Binder:	Thomson-Shore, Inc.
Text:	VIP Garamond
Display:	VIP Trump Medieval
Cloth:	Joanna Arrestox B 34620
Paper:	60 lb. P&S offset laid, B-32